The service-oriented enterprise

Enterprise-architecture and viable services

Tom Graves

Tetradian Consulting

Published by
Tetradian Books
Unit 215, Communications House
9 St Johns Street, Colchester, Essex CO2 7NN
England

http://www.tetradianbooks.com

First published January 2009
ISBN 978-1-906681-16-6 (paperback)
ISBN 978-1-906681-17-3 (e-book)

Contents

Acknowledgements

Amongst others, the following people kindly provided comments and feedback on the early drafts of this book: Daljit Banger (White Knight Consulting, GB), Shawn Callahan (Anecdote Pty Ltd, Aus), Charles Edwards (ProcessWave, GB), Geoff Elliott (St Neots, GB), Nigel Green (CapGemini, GB), Charles Millar (Marlow, GB), Kim Parker (AusPost, Aus), Liz Poraj-Wilczynska (Brockhampton, GB), Peter Tseglakof (AusPost, Aus), Jaco Vermeulen (Chaos Based, GB).

Please note that, to preserve commercial and personal confidentiality, the stories and examples in this book have been adapted, combined and in part fictionalised from experiences in a variety of contexts, and do not and are not intended to represent any specific individual or organisation.

Registered trademarks such as Zachman, TOGAF, FEAF, ITIL, ASL, BiSL etc are acknowledged as the intellectual property of the respective owners.

INTRODUCTION

The service-oriented enterprise

Everything in the enterprise is a service. Everything the enterprise does is a service. Everything the enterprise delivers is a service – even products are services, in a sense. And the enterprise itself is a service. *Everything* is a service.

That's the key idea behind the *service-oriented enterprise*: a view of the enterprise in which everything is seen in terms of services and their interactions and interdependencies, providing consistency and simplicity everywhere, and creating new space for agility and innovation in the enterprise.

This book explores why and how to put that idea into practice, with real business benefits across the entire enterprise.

Who should read this book?

The book is intended for enterprise architects and others who deal with the practical implications of whole-of-enterprise issues.

It should also be useful for strategists and service-managers, and for anyone who works with 'pervasive' themes such as supply-chains, value-webs, quality, security, knowledge-sharing, business ethics and social responsibility, health, safety and environment.

What's in this book?

The text is divided into three main sections:

- *Basics* (see *Basics – An overview*, p. 3) – reviewing key terms such as 'enterprise architecture' and 'service-oriented architecture', and the core metaphors underlying the service-oriented enterprise
- *Principles* (see *Principles – An overview*, p.29) – describing core ideas about the structure and relationships between services, and their relationship to the structure of the enterprise
- *Practice* (see *Practice – An overview*, p.92) – illustrating how to apply the principles in real-world business contexts, using a Functional Business Model as the anchor for the enterprise service-map, process-tree, costing-model and other variants

1

Each section contains several chapters, as smaller chunks to apply straight away in your day-to-day work. Although there's a fair amount of theory, the keyword here is *practice*: the aim is to give you something that you can *use*.

So each chapter includes examples and stories to place the ideas into a real-life context, with references to other relevant resources. Most chapters include or end with one or more 'Applications' sections, with questions to help you apply the material within your own context; and a 'Resources' section, pointing to sources for further information. There's also a glossary at the end of the book, which should help in clarifying the broader meaning of some of the common terms used in the architecture of the service-oriented enterprise.

But first, what *is* the service-oriented enterprise? To answer that, we need to explore some basic terms such as 'enterprise architecture' and 'service-oriented architecture'; and, behind that, the underlying metaphors that we use to describe the enterprise.

BASICS – AN OVERVIEW

Before we get into the meat of the issues, there are a few background items we need to address.

One of these is the role of enterprise architecture (see *Basics – Enterprise architecture*, p.5). At present, this field is often regarded as a subset of IT, and specifically of IT governance. But it makes far more sense if we extend it outward to its more literal meaning as the architecture of the enterprise as a whole.

Enterprise architecture is about the structure and purpose of the enterprise – how everything fits together in support of the enterprise vision and values and shorter-term goals. Viewing an enterprise entirely in terms of services is one of the more valuable ways to assess that structure, especially as it provides consistency between every part and every level within the enterprise.

A service-oriented architecture also starts to make more sense from that point of view (see *Basics – Service-oriented architecture*, p.11). As with enterprise-architecture, it initially arose as a way to resolve issues around detail-level IT: but here we expand its scope outward, as an architectural style to understand the entire enterprise in terms of service structures and content, and their mutual interactions and interdependencies.

As part of this, we'll also need to introduce some basic themes and terminology from formal systems-theory. This isn't well-known in business as yet: unfortunate but understandable, because much of so-called 'hard-systems theory' is described in a complex, arcane mathematics that may well seem impenetrable – and, frankly, irrelevant – to most people in business. The type we need here, though, is the human-oriented 'soft-systems' approach, which is much more approachable, and more easily expressed in business terms for the real business context.

Beneath that distinction between 'hard-systems' and 'soft-systems' is a fundamental difference in underlying metaphor, in the overall way we describe the enterprise (see *Basics – A matter of metaphor*, p.21). There's a key contrast here between the notion of 'enterprise as machine' – probably *the* most common business metaphor since the days of Frederick Taylor's 'scientific management', at the end of the nineteenth century – and the more recent concept of 'enterprise as living organism'. The mechanistic view has some real value at the detail-level of technology and process-design, but it simply does not work when we try to apply it to the whole enterprise – as many business-folk have discovered the hard way, in expensive debacles such as the failure of so many attempts at IT-based 'business process re-engineering'. Instead, if we are to gain the full value from a service-oriented architecture, we need to shift towards the more holistic, all-encompassing view of the 'living enterprise' model.

Enterprise architecture, service-oriented architecture, and a shift in underlying metaphor: together, these form the basic background for the service-oriented enterprise.

Resources

- Tom Graves, *Real Enterprise Architecture: beyond IT to the whole enterprise*, (Tetradian, 2008)
- Tom Graves, *Bridging the Silos: enterprise architecture for IT-architects* (Tetradian, 2008)
- Tom Graves, *Power and Response-ability: the human side of systems* (Tetradian, 2008)

4

BASICS – ENTERPRISE ARCHITECTURE

Summary

Enterprise architecture is a formal discipline managing a body of knowledge about the purpose and structure of an enterprise. It has its roots in IT systems and technology-management, but has steadily extended its scope towards covering the whole enterprise – and it will need that much broader scope if it is to fully describe the requirements of the service-oriented enterprise.

Details

What is enterprise architecture?

What *is* the enterprise? What holds it together? What structures do we need to make it work better, to help it adapt to its changing circumstances and business environment?

These are the core questions underlying the formal discipline of enterprise architecture. It's still a new discipline: the term itself was coined barely a decade ago, building on previous ideas about 'information systems architecture' and the like. There are several standards and formats – TOGAF (The Open Group Architecture Framework), FEAF (US Federal Enterprise Architecture Framework) and the Zachman framework being some of the best-known examples. Which leads us, though, to ask: what *is* an 'enterprise'? For that matter, what is meant by 'architecture' in this context?

An all-too-common answer to that last question – typified by the comments of the architecture manager at a recent client – would be "IT functions and data". When I explained that the business of her employer – a government department in the social-services sector – was a great deal wider than that, and hence her architecture needed to cover people-based processes, legislation and a great deal more, she replied, "Yes, I agree with you: architecture is all about IT functions and data". We went round that loop a couple more times before I gave up: there wasn't much point in trying to discuss real enterprise-architecture with someone who wouldn't allow herself to hear about any aspect of business beyond her own domain of IT. Oh well...

In every form of architecture – building architecture, naval architecture, process architecture, business architecture, whatever – the real focus is on structure, and the *use* of that structure. In the architecture and design of a hospital, for example, we would be as concerned with the workflows and other usage-patterns *within* the hospital as its physical framework of walls and wiring, passageways and plumbing. The same is true of enterprise architecture: it's about structure – *any* kind of structure within the enterprise, from data-definitions to downpipes and dumper-trucks - and the principles and guidelines that govern the *use* of that structure.

So what then is an enterprise? According to the FEAF specification, it's any kind of entity "supporting a defined business scope and mission", within which the various members or components "must coordinate their functions and share information" to achieve that purpose. The 'enterprise' might be a commercial business; it might be government or non-profit; it might be the local football club or the village New Mothers group; it actually doesn't matter what the size or purpose might be, as long as there is a defined scope and mission to share.

Note, though, that whilst an organisation is a kind of enterprise, not every enterprise is delimited by the legal and other boundaries of an organisation. *An enterprise may be any subset or superset of the organisation*: the IT department is an enterprise in its own right, within the overall enterprise of the parent organisation; a multi-partner cross-industry consortium is likewise an enterprise made up of a shared 'mission and scope' to which a group of smaller enterprises choose to align. There's no inherent restriction there: and in some cases the effective boundaries of the enterprise may well change from minute to minute.

Under those circumstances, governance of the enterprise can get complicated, to say the least. Which is where enterprise architecture comes into the picture:

Enterprise architecture is a discipline through which an enterprise can identify, develop and maintain its knowledge of its purpose, its structure and itself.

Enterprise architecture identifies and monitors the structures needed to support that shared mission; it assists in managing change, and responses to change; it provides guidance and consistency across the whole scope.

But here we may hit up against a problem of divergence between what is commonly thought to be the scope of enterprise architecture, and the real scope it needs to have. We need to address that issue of scope before we can move on.

The scope of architecture

In most current descriptions, 'enterprise architecture' is associated almost entirely with IT – in effect, the term is a kind of shorthand for 'enterprise-wide IT architecture'. But with each new stage of maturity, the scope has needed to expand further, from low-level technology and interfaces, to structures for data and applications, and then to a somewhat belated recognition that all of this needed to be linked to and driven from business strategy.

Yet all of this is still centred solely on IT: much so-called 'business architecture', for example, is often just an IT-oriented summary of 'everything not-IT'. So a typical view of the scope of that 'enterprise architecture' would be as in the TOGAF specification:

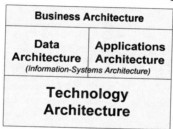

The IT-architecture hierarchy

Note the relative sizes of each area of interest in that diagram. In the original TOGAF-8 methodology, for example, assessment of low-level technology is assigned more than six times as many development steps as for the whole of the rest of the business put together. Kind of an imbalance there…

Every enterprise is different, yet very few are as IT-centric as the standard enterprise-architecture models suggest. And for the rest? Perhaps the simplest way is to describe each enterprise in terms of four distinct dimensions, which we could summarise as the four classic ways an enterprise distinguishes itself from its competitors:

- through *products and services* – a *physical* dimension of actions and transactions, "the way we do things round here"
- through *knowledge and innovation* – a *conceptual* dimension of ideas and information, "what we know, how we think"

- through *relationships and 'feel'* – a *relational* dimension of people and their individual skills and experience, "how we relate with each other, and with others"
- through *vision and purpose* – an *aspirational* dimension about direction, focus, morale, belonging, "who we are and what we stand for"

The FEAF reference-model describes these respectively as 'Other Fixed Assets', 'Technology' (by which they mean IT, though that's actually only a subset of knowledge-technology), 'Human Capital' and 'Business'. These dimensions interweave as the distinct and distinctive nature of the enterprise as a whole. So the layering of a *real* enterprise architecture would look more like this:

	Purpose *(Aspirational dimension)* **Business Architecture**		IT domain *(typical)*
People Systems-Architecture	**Information/Knowledge Systems-Architecture**	**Machine / Asset Systems-Architecture**	
Manual-Process Detail-Architecture	**Information-Process Detail-Architecture** *(Technology Architecture)*	**Machine-Process Detail-Architecture**	
People *(Relational dimension)*	Knowledge *(Conceptual dimension)*	Assets / 'Things' *(Physical dimension)*	

Whole-of-enterprise structure

So enterprise architecture isn't about IT – or rather, since IT does play a part in most present-day enterprises, it's not *only* about IT, but about how *every* aspect of the enterprise interacts with everything else. And it isn't centred on IT: it isn't centred anywhere, other than on that guiding theme, the 'defined business scope and mission'. In short:

The scope of enterprise architecture is always the whole of the enterprise – the enterprise *as* a whole

We may choose, for practical reasons, to set suitable limits on the scope of an architectural assessment or design. But the moment we forget that that's an arbitrary choice, not a fact, we'd be in trouble straight away: the real scope – *always* – is the whole of the enterprise.

The purpose of architecture

But what's the point of all of this? What's the *purpose* of enterprise architecture? To answer that, we need to return to the FEAF definition, that an enterprise has various members and components that coordinate their functions and share information to express or achieve their shared 'mission' or vision. The architecture provides a means to support that process of coordination; it provides consistency across the whole of the enterprise scope, and a consistent *description* of that scope.

That's the function of reference-frameworks: TOGAF's 'Integrated Information Infrastructure Reference Model' is one such generic example for the IT industry, whilst eTOM and SID ('enhanced Telecom Operations Model' and 'Structured Information/Data') are a matching pair for telecommunications service-providers, and SCOR (Supply-Chain Operations Reference-model) describes logistics and other supply-chain services.

But these are all fairly static models: they describe structure, but not much about interactions between the components of those structures. And they don't explain much about the *human* side of the systems – such as the so-called 'tacit' knowledge that resides only in people's heads, and is most often shared through stories and action-based learning. For these, we need a broader view of the structure, the system and the scope.

That's what a 'services' view of the architecture can provide for us. Services present a consistent frame through which to understand structure; and service-choreography describes the *use* of that structure. Which leads us, in turn, to a service-oriented view of the enterprise as a whole – the *service-oriented enterprise*.

That in turn would depend on a view of 'service-orientation' that's as broad as the scope of the enterprise itself. But as with 'enterprise architecture', the term is at present strongly associated with IT alone – too strongly for our needs here. To make this work, we need first to take a detour to find the *real* meaning of 'service-oriented architecture'.

Application

- What are the bounds of 'the enterprise' in your own business context? Are they a subset of the organisation; synonymous with the organisation; or do they extend beyond the organisation itself? What are the dynamics of those bounds – in what ways do they change, and for what purposes?

- Does your organisation maintain some kind of enterprise architecture? If so, what is its current scope? Where within the organisation does it reside? Who has responsibility for its scope and governance?

- If your existing enterprise-architecture is restricted to an IT-centric scope, what would need to be done to extend that to a true enterprise-wide scope? What can *you* do to assist in that change?
- What support does enterprise-architecture provide to enhance consistency across the enterprise? In what ways could that support be further enhanced within your enterprise?

Resources

- TOGAF (The Open Group Architecture Framework): see www.opengroup.org/togaf
- FEAF (US Federal Enterprise Architecture Framework): see www.gao.gov/special.pubs/eaguide.pdf [PDF]
- Zachman framework: see www.zifa.com
- Agile architecture development: see www.agileea.org
- Whole-of-enterprise architecture: see Tom Graves, *Real Enterprise Architecture: beyond IT to the whole enterprise,* (Tetradian, 2008)
- Adapting existing architecture-tools for whole-of-enterprise architecture: see Tom Graves, *Bridging the Silos: enterprise architecture for IT-architects* (Tetradian, 2008)

BASICS – SERVICE-ORIENTED ARCHITECTURE

Summary

As with enterprise architecture, service-oriented architecture has to date been associated almost exclusively with low-level IT. We can break free from that restriction, and open out to the whole scope of enterprise architecture, by recognising that *everything* in the enterprise provides a service.

Details

Services and IT-architecture

If we read the existing literature on service-oriented architecture – the Wikipedia summary, say – we'll find the same as with enterprise architecture: it seems it's all about low-level IT, and nothing else. And as with enterprise architecture, it's not the whole story: the IT is only a small part of the enterprise. Yet it's often the only part that most people know, so it's probably the best place to start: we just have to remember to translate any IT-centric assumptions to the broader whole-of-enterprise scope.

In IT-architecture, a *service* is a composite made up of small blocks of functionality that collectively present a unified interface – often but not always a single interface – to the 'external' world, and are otherwise *autonomous*, ideally with no 'hard-wired' links to any other services. Some of the other key ideas include:

- *loosely coupled* – services have minimal dependence on each other: "services share schema and contract, not class", to quote one of the original services theorists, Don Box
- *contract-based* – the service to be delivered is defined in a 'service description document', or some other kind of 'contract' or service-level agreement
- *discoverable* – the service and its interface-contract – including information on the *quality* available in the contract, to aid process optimisation – should be identifiable automatically

11

- *abstraction* – as long as the service delivers in accordance with the specified interface-contract, how it does what it does should be a 'black box', internal detail that is (mostly) irrelevant to the user of the service
- *reusable* and *composable* – the service should be designed for re-use in a variety of different ways and in aggregations into larger blocks of shared functionality
- *interchangeable* – it should be possible to switch between services on different systems and from different service-providers that adhere to the same nominal service-contract specification

Overall, this gives some great advantages:

- we break free from monolithic, hardwired 'applications' that are cumbersome, fragile and hard to change
- developers can optimise the internal mechanisms of a service without affecting its exposed interface
- we can 'mix and match' between services to create new 'mashups' for rapid response to business change
- services can be described in business terms, enabling people without an IT background to create their own personalised mashups
- we can call on the facilities of multiple service-providers for the same nominal service, for load-balancing and risk-management, or for business reasons such as reduced costs or faster response

All good: but there *are* some significant downsides, which at times may be overlooked amidst the flood of marketing-hype. There's a sense sometimes of a wishful attitude of 'build it and they will come': yet in a true service-oriented architecture, services have no inherent context, they just *are*. So issues around 'discoverability' – self-advertising, in effect – suddenly become non-trivial: a concern that barely existed with the old monolithic applications, where every function was hardwired into the run-time code.

Also unlike those monolithic applications, there's no inherent built-in mechanism that links services together into processes: that choreography has to come from somewhere beyond the services themselves. And the need for service-contracts can bring a hefty overhead in terms of bandwidth and execution-time, especially where service-connections need to be created in real-time.

A service-orientation for IT-architecture enables new options, new possibilities: one such example is 'cloud-computing', in which IT-services can be exchanged and accessed from anywhere across the web. Yet all of this is still solely from the IT perspective. Once we look wider, and extend the scope of a service-oriented architecture, we start to see that there are other advantages, and other challenges – some of them subtle, even strange, perhaps, but all of which *do* need to be addressed.

Security and other service challenges

Probably the greatest challenges to a service-oriented architecture revolve around security. Every access to anything will require some kind of identity-management:

- Is this requester who they claim to be?
- If they are, do they have the appropriate 'need to know, need to use'?
- If it's a commercial service, do they have access to the funds to pay for the service?
- How do we confirm all of this, within the response-time specified in the service-contract?

In a typical monolithic application, we would control access to information or functions via some kind of token. Once someone has logged into some system, we can use that token to track anything they do and ask for within the bounds of that system, and respond accordingly. Often all we'll need to do is something like a lookup to a list of passwords and a list of matching access-rights, and we'd be all but done: problem solved. For the enterprise as a whole, almost the only complications are the need to get people to change their passwords from time to time, to reduce the risk that security may be compromised; and the need to align access-controls for the various different monolithic systems that people need to use – hence the 'holy grail' of a so-called 'single sign-on' for every system, which sounds simple enough in theory, if not so simple in practice...

But in a service-oriented model, identify-management is suddenly *much* more complicated – especially on the internet, which has no built-in mechanism to track 'stateful' concerns such as identity and security. 'The system' – such as it is – consists of layer upon layer of near-arbitrary collections of "small pieces loosely joined": we can pass around a token, perhaps, but as yet there's no quick, simple, automatic means to link that token to any central register of access-rights. And once we're outside the enterprise firewall – as we would be with most cloud-computing services, for example – we have to deal with all the security nightmare of the internet, with hacking, spoofing, interception, forged identity and the rest: it's not a pretty picture.

> The technical challenges of SOA are almost trivial compared to its security challenges: there's good reason why all of the recent Open Group conferences on enterprise-architecture have also featured a major stream on security and service-architecture. The catch is that many of the issues are have little or nothing to do with IT – a fact which can be difficult for the many people who turn up at such conferences with an IT-only background, a fixed IT-centric view of the business world, and an equally fixed assumption that every possible problem has an IT-based solution... But unless we *do* think wider about security than just the IT, we're likely to cause more problems than we solve: when security is our responsibility, we're responsible for *all* of it, not just the easy part that's well within our comfort-zone!

Another classic problem in service-choreography is what's known as 'deadly embrace'. An example from the hardwired computer-systems of a few decades ago would be where one service gains exclusive access to a datastore, and then requests the printer, at the same time as another service locks the printer for its use and then requests the datastore. Each service is then stuck waiting for the other: which would not be popular with the services' users...

In principle, and in direct form, at least that kind of problem has long since been resolved with tactics such as asynchronous printer-queues and optimistic record-locking; and the sheer speed of most present-day data-processing also helps. But each service-transaction takes *time* to set up, especially through all those world-wide routing-mechanisms of the internet; and when we have to wade our way through layer upon layer of access-control services and suchlike to get anything done, the total set-up time may well exceed that for the actual transaction many times over. And that's assuming that everything works: it's not always obvious what will happen when any service-transaction fails within an overall choreography. So even if it's not a true 'deadly embrace' in a technical sense, it may well feel like it... And when such a widely-distributed system fails in that way, it's often far from obvious as to whose responsibility it would be to fix it: which is guaranteed trouble at a business level. So cloud-computing may sound almost perfect in principle, perhaps, but may not be so perfect in practice.

And then there are a whole swathe of other issues that have little or nothing to do with IT as such, but can have serious impacts on IT-based services. For example, almost every country has its own distinct and different rules around privacy, record-keeping and the like. So whilst in principle data could be stored anywhere in the world, many countries mandate that some (but *only* some) information should never cross national borders – which means that service-users must have proof from service-providers that that is indeed the case.

Other countries – particularly the US – assert legal concerns about restricting information to their own citizens only – who may, however, be anywhere in the world. Then there are the thorny issues around pornography and the like, where access may be limited not by nationality but by age, or other personal attributes. All of which lead to chaotic confusions about who can and can't see what, and who has authority and responsibility to control such limitations – let alone, again, dealing with all the hackers and spoofers and suchlike. Messy indeed.

A true service-oriented architecture needs to be able to deal with every one of these issues. Which is not straightforward at all. Which is why a service-based view of the enterprise needs also to be strongly linked to a solid structure for service-management – not just for IT, but for the whole of the enterprise.

Services and service-management

Whether in 'cloud-computing' or in old-style applications, IT services need to be linked together into end-to-end business processes – which means there needs to be something above the services themselves to create that choreography. In the same way, there also needs to be an IT infrastructure on which the services will run. The latter would be more the realm of IT-architecture, perhaps, but all of this would come under the general heading of 'service management'.

Probably *the* international standard for IT service-management is ITIL, the 'IT Infrastructure Library' developed by the UK Office of Government Commerce. So in this context it's interesting to compare two versions of that standard: Version 2, published in 2004, and the Version 3 update, released in 2007.

ITIL v2 uses a classic IT-centric 'them and us' model for its overview. On the far left there's 'The Business'; on the far right, 'The Technology'. Between them sits the core of service-management,

Service Delivery and Service Support, with an interface of The Business Perspective on one side and ICT Infrastructure Management on the other. Above and below we have a useful focus on planning, on application-management, on ever-essential security-management. That's it, apart from an emphasis throughout on 'IT/Business alignment' – though it's never very clear about who is supposed to align with whom.

ITIL v3 is radically different: there's almost no IT-centrism at all. In principle it's all about service-management for IT, but apart from a few low-level technical details we could remove the term 'IT' throughout and it would still make perfect sense. It starts with Service Strategy; moves on to Service Design; then Service Transition, about implementing those designs; and Service Operation. Interweaving all of those is Continual Service Improvement. Each is "a set of specialised organisational capabilities for providing value to customers in the form of services", with an emphasis on managing the overall service lifecycle as much as service delivery and support. And though never stated explicitly, perhaps the real key point in ITIL is this:

Service-management is itself a service:
it delivers the services of service-management

The ITIL standard describes those service-management services, and the *relationships* between those services, both in terms of their interdependencies and choreography, and in terms of the mutual responsibilities over time. But it also helps us to think about services in much broader terms than those of IT architecture alone. Which matters, because ultimately, *everything* is a service.

Everything is a service

Whatever it looks like, and whatever form it may take, *everything* in an enterprise delivers a service. That's the real implication of a service-oriented architecture; and also the real reason for its importance to the enterprise.

Everything is a service. Even products are proto-services, in a sense, because they provide the end-customer with the means to deliver a self-service: a vacuum-cleaner provides the service of cleaned floors, the grocery-shopping provides the self-service of meals, and so on. "Customers do not buy products", says the ITIL v3 specification, "they buy the satisfaction of particular needs". And we satisfy those needs through the services we provide.

Shifting the perspective from products to services can be more profitable, too. Interface Inc is one of the world's leading manufacturers of flooring materials, and some two decades ago, in the words of its founder Ray Anderson, was consuming "an ocean of petroleum" each year to make its products. It was a profitable enterprise, if perhaps not as profitable as it could have been – though with the 'business as usual' mindset of the time, it was far from clear as to what needed to change to make that quantum shift in profitability.

But in the late-1990s Anderson had what he called "a spear to the chest" – a kind of double-epiphany about sustainability. One side of it was a recognition that every scrap of waste – at that time a huge problem for the corporation – was something that they'd paid for but couldn't sell. Hence zero-waste was not merely a 'feel-good' goal, but a *business* matter with serious business impacts: waste-reduction leads directly to more profit, and *everyone* wins. At the present time, Interface is about halfway towards its 'Mission Zero' goal for the year 2020 – zero waste, zero environmental impact, everything recycled – and its profitability continues to climb with each passing year.

Anderson's other 'epiphany' was a realisation about a link between products, services and waste. Interface had sold carpet and other flooring *products*; but what its clients really wanted – 'the satisfaction of a particular need' – was the *service* of covered floors: and to the end-customer, that service had higher value *as* a service. So Interface started to shift their business that way – and discovered that to make it work, they also had to shift their attitude to waste. When the company was oriented towards products, it was in their interest to get their customers to be careless about waste: more waste equals more product sold, and built-in obsolescence seems like a good idea, too. But it's the other way round when the company embeds the product in its own fixed-fee service: suddenly it's in the company's interest for customers to *minimise* their waste, and for products to be as durable as possible. So for the service-oriented enterprise, sustainability is good business in every sense – and once again, *everyone* wins.

In IT service-oriented architecture, we rethink IT functions and the like in terms of services. But in the service-oriented enterprise, we take that idea a stage further, and rethink *everything* in service terms. Service-management is a service; management is a service; so is strategy, architecture, the office canteen. Everything in the entire enterprise is a service.

In ITIL v3, a service is defined in rather abstract terms, as a means of delivering value by facilitating the customer's desired outcomes. The service is both valued and valuable because we take on some of the complexity and risk on the customer's behalf. And the service is accorded a value by the customer to the extent that it makes those outcomes easier to achieve.

Product is about 'what'; service is about 'how' and 'who' and 'where' and 'when'; but what the customer is *really* interested in is their 'why' – and often don't greatly care about how that 'why' can be achieved, as long it *is* achieved with the minimum of difficulty and fuss. As a service-provider, that's *our* desired outcome: a satisfied customer. In a commercial context, satisfaction *matters* – because a satisfied customer is likely to come back for more.

Incidentally, this is one point where 'black box' encapsulation of service-internals may cross over with demands for transparency, giving a much more subtle definition of 'customer satisfaction'.

When the Australian 'Ghan' railway line from Adelaide to Darwin was upgraded some years back, one of the tenders was presented by a Chinese consortium. Unlike the other tenders, which assumed a relatively small workforce and large amounts of heavy machinery, the Chinese proposed instead to use a vast manual workforce of *half a million* labourers. The delivered service-*results* would have been exactly the same, created to the same nominal service-level agreement. The Chinese proposal even worked out cheaper – even allowing for the logistics of serving that workforce in difficult near-desert conditions – hence would have been much 'better' than the other tenders if the price had been the only criterion.

But an end-customer may well be concerned with more than just the end-result. That was certainly true in this case: the politics were *way* too scary, for a start – especially as that imported workforce would represent a significant percentage of the country's entire population. So sometimes the simple black-box encapsulation can risk *reducing* 'customer satisfaction'. In an IT service-oriented architecture we might not need to take account of such issues, but at the whole-of-enterprise level we certainly do.

Something else to think about, anyway.

In the service-oriented enterprise, every activity has an explicitly-identified customer to whom that service has value; and each of those customers has an outcome that they want to achieve. Those two points *define* the service-need, and hence the structure and nature of the service.

Perhaps more to the point, if we *can't* identify the customer and their need, we're probably delivering a service that has no value – a situation which is far from uncommon in larger enterprises, particularly in the myriad of performance reports created with so much effort but that no-one ever actually reads...

Do beware, though, of the common mistake of attempting to define that value solely in monetary terms. We can't *eat* money; we can't travel with money alone; we can't get a hug from it, or a greeting

---

> home; it doesn't even make a good floor-covering. Money is a *means* to an outcome – not the outcome itself. To make a service-oriented architecture work, we need to be clear about what that outcome is – not just the means by which we get there.

Products enable services; and services in turn enable outcomes. As a service-provider, delivery of the service is the endpoint of all our work; but from the customer's perspective, the service is only a means to an end – it's not *in itself* their intended outcome. To understand the service-need, we must describe that outcome in *business* terms, and usually distinct from the service itself. To use an example from the ITIL v3 specification, we ourselves might think of our service as delivering 'an online sales-information process' or suchlike; but what our service-customer actually wants is something that will enable their sales-people to spend more time face-to-face with their own customers. *That's* the real need; *that's* what we need to design our service for; *that's* the real measure of 'success' in service terms – a satisfied customer. How we get to that desired outcome is up to us: to a large extent, the client doesn't want to know, as long as the outcome *is* achieved.

Which brings us back to those core principles of service-oriented architecture: loosely-coupled, contract-based, discoverable, interchange, abstraction and so on. Those support best-value for the customer. Other principles support best-value for *us* as service-providers: particularly reusability, composability and, again, a layered abstraction. But these depend in turn, on that fundamental shift in perspective: that *everything* in the enterprise is a service.

It's not an easy shift in perspective, perhaps, but the payoffs can be huge – especially in terms of simplicity, clarity, resilience and speed of response to change. Yet to make it work well, we need another parallel shift in perspective, about the way we view the enterprise *as* a whole. And that shift is what we need to look at next.

Application

- What to you is 'service-oriented architecture'? How would you apply such ideas in your existing enterprise?
- How do you address the security and identity-management issues in service-oriented architecture? And the synchronous-transaction issues?

- What structures and processes do you use for service-management? Do they only apply to IT-services, or to other services as well?
- Who are the clients for your services? How do you identify and model their business needs and business outcomes? How do you ensure that your services deliver against those outcomes?
- What distinctions do you currently draw between products and services? Who are the users and 'consumers' of each? In what ways do those users differ, in terms of expectations, responsibilities and so on?

Resources

- Service-oriented IT-architecture: see Wikipedia summary at en.wikipedia.org/wiki/Service_oriented_architecture
- ITIL (Information Technology Infrastructure Library): see www.itil.org.uk and www.itil-officialsite.com
- BiSL (Business Information Services Library) and ASL (Application Services Library): see www.aslbislfoundation.org
- Ray Anderson and the Interface Inc story: see www.interfaceinc.com/who/founder.html and www.interfaceglobal.com

BASICS – A MATTER OF METAPHOR

Summary

The most common metaphor for the enterprise is to view it as some kind of complicated yet controllable machine. But to succeed with a whole-of-enterprise architecture that is based on services, we have to shift our perspective, and view the enterprise more as a kind of living organism in its own right, with its own self-chosen direction and purpose.

Details

Machine and organism

For at least a hundred years, the dominant metaphor of business has been that of 'enterprise as machine'. The science behind its notion of 'scientific management' is essentially Newtonian, a clockwork universe following implacable, supposedly universal 'laws of business'. And there's no doubt that it did work well, for the business-owners at least: Ford's assembly-lines were hailed as marvels of their age, as productivity leapt many-fold under the ever-vigilant eye of the time-and-motion man.

But times have moved on: despite the evident desire of so many managers to cling on to the apparent certainties of the past, it's clear that the old-style 'scientific management' has long passed its own 'use-by' date. It's not wrong, as such: but in practice it's a special case, one that only works well in stable markets with stable products and slow rates of change – a business context which these days has become a relative rarity, an almost unheard-of luxury. To cope with the complexities of the real business world of the present, we need an approach which is much more flexible, much more resilient, much faster in response to change.

And if the times have moved on, so has the underlying science. A new version of Taylor's 'scientific management' would have to include complexity-science, systems-theory, emergence, ecology – and living systems. To understand service-oriented architecture and the true nature of the service-oriented enterprise, a better

21

metaphor is not 'enterprise as machine', but 'enterprise as living organism'. But the 'machine' view is still so dominant in present-day business that it's worthwhile spending some time to explore the differences between these two core metaphors.

Structural basis

In the machine metaphor, the enterprise is comprised of a myriad of small components. To work well, all of these components must mesh together, like gears inside a machine. Every part must be carefully designed, engineered and machined to fit in its allotted place – in *only* that place – and is interchangeable with any other matching part. Every task has a predefined 'job-description': the machine has no real place for skill, and individual difference is almost anathema. Everything is a 'resource': hence the term 'human resources' – and hence too that bitter sense of feeling regarded as no more than 'a cog in the machine', to be discarded on the scrap-heap as soon as our work is done.

In the organism metaphor, the enterprise is composed of a myriad of interdependent services, working together, as a community, towards a common purpose. Although there is some specialisation – giving the appearance of radical difference in some cases – each of the cells ultimately shares the same underlying structure. The network of interdependencies is such that the overall structure, and even the cells within it, will automatically adapt itself to change, and will spread the load in the event of damage. No part, however, is *directly* interchangeable with any other. Replacement will naturally occur, but the whole organism changes with each: and what keeps the organism together under such change is that unifying purpose.

Location of purpose

In the machine metaphor, the key point is that the machine has no inherent or intrinsic purpose: it's just a machine. Any purpose for the machine has to come from outside of the machine itself. In the classic Victorian model, the machine – and hence everything and everyone in it – exists to serve the purpose of whoever is declared to be its 'owner': the shareholders, in the present-day version of that model. In the commercial context, its purpose is as a 'machine for making money'. The means and mechanisms by which it does so are apparently almost irrelevant, as long it does so to the owners' satisfaction; if not, the machine itself may be discarded, at whim.

22

In the organism metaphor, a shared purpose is fundamental to the existence of the organism. Purpose is *intrinsic*, not extrinsic: it comes from within the enterprise, not from outside. Means and mechanisms all need to align with that purpose in order to work well; and in essence, the organism owns itself.

> One of the practical difficulties of the organism metaphor in a present-day commercial context is that it *doesn't* align well with the 'shareholder-as-owner' model. As business commentator Charles Handy put it, "Companies today are quintessentially collections of people adding value to material things. It is not appropriate to 'own' collections of people. Particularly it is inappropriate for anonymous outsiders to own these far from anonymous people."
>
> In short, the organism metaphor exposes the bleak fact that the current shareholder model asserts purported 'ownership rights' that, in human terms, are dangerously close to slavery – which is *not* a stable or sustainable basis for any economy…

Structure of management

In the machine metaphor, management is a 'thing apart': it exists to control the machine, on behalf of the 'owners', but is separate and distinct from both. There's an almost absolute split between 'brain' and 'brawn', often seen as an clash of opposites – management *versus* workers, white-collar *versus* blue-collar. Knowledge is deemed to reside *only* in management: the machine is brainless in itself – a 'mere machine'. So all of its necessary thinking must be done by 'outsiders', whilst control of the implementation of that thinking is distributed throughout the machine via a hierarchy of authority: the classic management-textbook distinctions between 'staff' and 'line'.

In the organism metaphor, management is simply another service: it's intrinsic to every part of the enterprise. There's no inherent separation between 'brain' and 'brawn' – indeed, the organism would fail if its brain were to be excised in the same way as in the machine-metaphor. Knowledge, and the ability to garner and apply that knowledge, are all likewise distributed throughout the organism, with an emphasis on local knowledge applied to the local context. Management exists to support and guide, but does not attempt to control.

> Most modern models for quality-management take this approach: for example, one of the core principles is that the knowledge to solve a problem in manufacturing is most likely to come from those who are closest to the work.

The catch is that this is almost the exact opposite view to the 'machine-metaphor' management-knows-best model that's still preferred – perhaps unsurprisingly – by so many middle-managers. But W Edwards Deming, one of the figureheads of the quality movement, was insistent – and unrepentant – on this point: most of the problems in quality had their roots in the structural failings of the management system, he said, and managers should look to their own behaviours first before blaming front-line workers for poor quality. Although he doesn't describe it in such terms, Deming's work provides one of the best descriptions of how the 'living organism' metaphor applies in real practice, especially in the manufacturing context. Strongly recommended.

Emphasis for overall improvement

In the machine metaphor, the main interests in improvement are about efficiency and reliability. Efficiency is seen as 'doing more with less' – which in a business context usually means cutting costs, and cutting costs, and cutting costs yet again, in a relentless quest for the nirvana of getting everything for nothing. Reliability is supposedly important too, though in practice it often comes a distant second in priority to an imagined 'efficiency'.

In the organism metaphor, efficiency and reliability are recognised as two of the five factors in *effectiveness* – 'efficient on purpose':

- *efficient*: makes the best use of the available resources
- *reliable*: can be relied on to deliver the required results
- *elegant*: supports the human factors in the context
- *appropriate*: supports and sustains the overall purpose
- *integrated*: linked to and supports integration of the whole *as* whole

In the 'living enterprise', performance depends on how well we *optimise* all the trade-offs across these dimensions that, together, express the enterprise's 'ability to do work'. Efficiency is neither the same as effectiveness, nor separate from it, but is a *subset* of what's needed for overall effectiveness. So improvements focus on the *balance* between these dimensions – not solely on a single theme such as efficiency.

These themes of enterprise effectiveness are explored in more depth in two other books in this series: *Real Enterprise Architecture: beyond IT to the whole enterprise* and *SEMPER and SCORE: enhancing enterprise effectiveness* – see the 'Resources' section below.

Resilience and change

In the machine metaphor, there can be no inherent resilience as such: the enterprise is just a machine, with very limited options to adapt itself to change. The purpose, the brain and even most of the senses are all 'external': adaptation for change can only come from outside – hence the armies of self-styled 'management consultants'. The process of change is typified by such mechanistic terms as 'restructuring', 'business process re-engineering', or John Zachman's notion of 'engineering the enterprise'. Everything in the machine is an interchangeable component, so a typical change-process will consist of pulling the machine apart, and then re-assembling the components in a different order, according to some revised 'system design'. There is no real concept of human impact in any of this, because there's no real concept of people *as* people: they're 'human resources', no different from any other enterprise asset. The only obvious difficulty – from within that metaphor, at least – is that response to change is usually reactive and slow: the result is that there's an apparently limitless need to keep tinkering with the machine, always running to keep up with an ever-changing reality, a futile search for the final, certain, stable 'future state'.

In the organism metaphor, the mesh of interdependencies provides the enterprise with inherent resilience to sway with the winds of change. The notion of *viable services* – which we'll explore further throughout this book – means that the enterprise becomes *self*-adapting, guided overall by the defined business purpose; the whole focus is 'efficient *on purpose*'. The one serious difficulty posed by all that interdependence is that we can't pull the enterprise apart, in the same brutal way that we can in the machine-metaphor, and expect it to survive the change unscathed. If we truly do have to excise some part of the organism, we have to do so with a great deal of care.

> Mergers can be difficult enough for a large enterprise, but demergers are often worse. Following the same enterprise-as-organism metaphor, we could suggest that 'survivability' of such a split could depend on the complexity of the 'organism': amoebas split themselves apart as an everyday activity, but humans don't!
>
> In some cases there might be a useful analogy here with lizards that can regrow a tail; or with the axolotl, which can even regrow an entire missing limb; or also with so-called 'superorganisms' such as a beehive or an ant-nest, in which the 'organism' is itself composed of near-autonomous, semi-independent individuals.

> But the oddest and certainly most interesting analogy would be with the unfortunately-named slime-moulds. They start out as individuals barely bigger than an amoeba, but can merge together into a strange anarchic entity, a kind of gigantic single-cell creature, in some species up to a metre or more across, with many independent nuclei moving around inside it – metaphorically speaking, an enormous enterprise with a completely 'flat' management-structure. They have some similarities to fungi, but as a collective entity can move around in search of food, at speeds of almost a metre a minute – far faster than any individual cell. And when food runs out completely – or, metaphorically, when the collective enterprise finally fails – the whole thing splits apart again back into individual cells, which waft away into the breeze as microscopic spores, to start the cycle all over again. The ultimate demerger, perhaps...
>
> But the point here is that when we view the enterprise as organism, we recognise that whatever we do to change the enterprise, we can't just wrench it all apart without doing some serious damage: it has to be done with a great deal more subtlety and care than in the machine-metaphor's 're-engineering'.

Services in the living enterprise

In the machine-metaphor, we would typically describe units of the enterprise in terms of mechanistic *components*, linked together into larger and larger assemblies But in the organism metaphor, the natural descriptors are cells and *services*: layer upon layer of them, interacting, interweaving, interdependent services, each delivering something of vital service and value to the overall enterprise.

The machine-metaphor for the enterprise isn't wrong as such: it's just that it's too limited for what we really need, in order to understand the enterprise *as* enterprise, and how to work with it in an architectural sense. The machine-metaphor's components describe the *composition* of the enterprise; the organism-metaphor's services describe what it *does* and *is*, and who and how it serves.

As per that previous definition, an enterprise is a community of some kind, coordinating its actions and resources in support of some shared mission and purpose. And that purpose – 'that which it serves' – must always be greater than itself. Each service has a identifiable customer, with whom it shares a common 'higher purpose' – hence the need for the purpose to have a broader scope than that of the enterprise alone. As we move up the layers of services to reach the scope of 'the enterprise as a whole', we gain a broader yet more precise view of the ultimate 'higher purpose' for the enterprise.

Before we risk wandering off into the realms of religion and the rest, remember that all of this is still only a metaphor! Think of these descriptions as an 'as-if', not an 'is': it's just an analogy, not the thing itself.

The point is that both the enterprise and the customers for its services – whatever they may be – need some kind of shared 'higher purpose' in order to bond together for that exchange of services. The classic way to describe this is in terms of vision, role, mission and goal: the enterprise *vision* describes that common 'higher purpose', the *role* describes how the enterprise sees itself in relation to that purpose – in other words, the services it provides for that purpose – whilst the *mission* is the enterprise capabilities that underpin that role, and so on. We won't be covering much more about that particular layering here, but there's more detail on the 'visioning' process in the 'Architecture on purpose' chapter of this book's companion volume *Real Enterprise Architecture* – see the *Resources* section below.'

A simple organism is self-contained: it's *viable* within itself, but doesn't interact that much with other organisms – it doesn't offer or consume many services – and probably doesn't have much of a purpose, either. But even in a basic bacillus there's some special-isation within the structure, and this specialisation is replicated on larger and larger scales as we move upward in levels of organic complexity, with individual cells, then clusters of cells, then entire organs, providing the myriad of specialised services that the over-all organism – or enterprise – will need.

To make sense of how this works in the *viable enterprise*, we need some kind of overview or conceptual structure. So that's what we'll look at next, before going on to apply those principles in business practice.

Application

- In what ways do you describe the enterprise, or aspects of the enterprise, as parts of a machine? How is this reflected in the everyday language of the enterprise, such as 'operations', 'functions', 'business units' and the like?

- In what ways do you describe the enterprise, or aspects of the enterprise, as being some kind of living organism? How is this reflected in the everyday language of the enterprise, such as 'culture', 'health', 'taking the pulse', or even the term 'corporation' itself?

- What other metaphors do you use to describe the enterprise? How are these reflected in the everyday language of the enterprise, such as 'getting a green light' (a 'roads' metaphor), or 'taking a bet' (a metaphor of finance as gambling), or 'cooking up a new project', perhaps?

- What impact do such metaphors have on the operation and existence of your enterprise? In the short-term? Medium-term? Long-term?

Resources

🕸 Frederick Taylor and 'scientific management': see Wikipedia summary at en.wikipedia.org/wiki/Scientific_management

📖 'Living enterprise' metaphor: see Arie de Geus, *The Living Company* (Longview Publishing, 1997)

🕸 Principles of 'living enterprise': see www.livingorganisations.com/default.htm

📖 Charles Handy on corporate ownership: see essay 'A company possessed', in Charles Handy, *Beyond Certainty* (Arrow Books, 1996)

🕸 W Edwards Deming and quality: see Wikipedia summary at en.wikipedia.org/wiki/W._Edwards_Deming

📖 Enterprise architecture and effectiveness: see Tom Graves, *Real Enterprise Architecture: beyond IT to the whole enterprise* (Tetradian, 2008)

📖 Effectiveness at the whole-of-enterprise level: see Tom Graves, *SEMPER and SCORE: enhancing enterprise effectiveness* (Tetradian, 2008)

PRINCIPLES – AN OVERVIEW

The core principles of service-oriented architecture and design are well-documented from the work on IT-services:

- encapsulation of sub-components into bundles of more usable functionality
- loose-coupling via messages and standards
- service-contracts between 'requester' and 'provider' roles
- 'black box' abstraction of the internal workings of services
- design for reuse and re-purpose
- self-advertising of capabilities and interface needs, to enable 'discoverability'

As we move beyond detail-level IT, though, other concerns may also come into play. One is that there may need to be multiple implementations of a service, to allow for operational issues as such up-scaling, down-scaling and disaster-recovery. Another is that we need to be aware of the different types of services and how they interrelate with each other – see *Principles – The structure of services*, p.31. And we also need to be clear about the distinctions between the service-types themselves:

- services that provide the *deliverables* of the enterprise, or directly support those deliverables – see *Principles – Delivery services*, p.42
- services that *manage* the enterprise and its services – see *Principles – Management services*, p.49
- services that provide the *coordination* for end-to-end processes – see *Principles – Coordination services*, p.62
- services that promote, protect and preserve the *pervasive values* of the enterprise – see *Principles – Pervasive services*, p.71

We need to remember, too, that none of these services exists in isolation: every service has its own set of relationships and inter-dependencies, all interweaving through the 'value-web' that is the whole enterprise. To make sense of all of this from an architectural perspective, we need some means to clarify the complexity. The best way to do this is to describe the interactions in terms of architectural patterns, typically derived from formal systems-theory – see *Principles – Properties and patterns*, p.78.

This combination of structure, categorisation and patterns gives us a framework that we can apply in practice to real everyday architectural issues in the enterprise.

Resources

Services in IT-architecture: see Wikipedia summary at en.wikipedia.org/wiki/Service_Oriented_Architecture

Services in whole-of-enterprise architecture: see Tom Graves, 'The Viable Services Model: Service quality, service interdependence and service completeness' in Jan van Bon [ed.], *IT Service Management: Global best practices* (itSMF/Van Haren, 2008)

PRINCIPLES – THE STRUCTURE OF SERVICES

Summary

Starting from the machine-metaphor notion of a strict separation between management and workforce, 'brain' and 'brawn', we use Stafford Beer's 'Viable System Model' as a basic structure to describe services and their interrelationships within any layer of the enterprise.

Details

Brain and brawn

Architecture is about structure, and about the way that the various components fit together within that structure: so it's easy to see how most current styles of enterprise-architecture would naturally align themselves with a machine-metaphor for the enterprise. In that sense, the nature of architecture itself is part of the problem here.

Yet living entities have their structure too – though we do need to remember that it *is* a living entity, not a dead machine! So to extend that metaphor a little further, what is the anatomy of a service? Or its physiology?

Perhaps the simplest place to start is the machine-metaphor's split between 'brain' and 'brawn'. Even the simplest bacillus will show some internal specialisation, and by the time we get to a true stand-alone cell such as an amoeba, there's some definite structure there. In particular, there's a single distinct nucleus somewhere near the centre, which acts much like the entity's 'brain'; and a variety of smaller structures such as mitochondria, lysosomes and vacuoles scattered throughout the cytoplasm that provide various support-functions and act as the cell's 'brawn'.

The cell itself exists within a broader environment, in which it will serve some purpose, in an ecological sense at least. So in the abstract, hierarchical terms typified by classic 'scientific management', we could summarise this visually as follows:

31

'Brain' and 'brawn'

Extending the 'scientific management' view further into the business context, the cell-like service exists to serve the purpose set by the external 'owners':

Machine-metaphor model of a service

In anything larger than the most minimal organism, the cell exists within a hierarchy of larger cell-like structures that replicate on larger scales the specialisations that exist within each individual cell. So too in the enterprise: services are aggregated into larger-scale services, each encapsulating some specific functionality for the enterprise. Each service has its own 'customers', and its own role within the overall purpose; and the same is true for every sub-service, and sub-sub-service, and so on.

Yet the layering of services is such that the 'brain/brawn' pair of a single service becomes part of the 'brawn' for the next layer upward in the hierarchy. So here we meet one of the fundamental flaws in 'scientific management': it asserts an absolute split between white-collar and blue-collar, 'brain' and 'brawn', but in functional terms *'brain' and 'brawn' together form a single, indivisible unit.* 'Brain' cannot be regarded as something separate, but in effect is distributed throughout the entire enterprise, *interwoven* with its 'brawn'. If we try to treat them as separate, we break down that 'interwovenness': the service ceases to be viable – and with it, perhaps, the overall enterprise.

> By the nature of cell-anatomy, the machine-metaphor's separation of 'brain' and 'brawn' does sort-of work at the lowest 'cell-like' levels of the enterprise, and perhaps gives a pleasing illusion of control at the highest levels. Yet the metaphor's insistence on treating all 'brawn' as

brainless – and 'brain' likewise as 'brawnless' – will guarantee intractable problems anywhere in the middle, and ultimately renders the entire enterprise unworkable. As we can see all too easily in practice – but perhaps not so easily see *why*...

Looking at a single cell in a microscope, it's quite easy to identify the nucleus and the other individual sub-services. But it can be easy to forget that all of these sub-entities are enclosed within the one cell-wall, and operate *as a single unit*; and also easy to forget that each cell will usually be part of a larger structure, which itself will be part of a larger structure, and so on. And it's also easy to become distracted by the fact that within each cell, there will be many subsidiary services, and often many instances of a particular type of subsidiary service, yet just *one* nucleus, one 'brain'.

There are a few rare examples, such as the slime-moulds mentioned earlier, in which there may be multiple nuclei within the one overall cell – but we can safely leave them out of this discussion for now!

Given that apparent uniqueness, it's easy to see how management – the business equivalent of the cell's nucleus – would tend to think of itself as 'special and different'. That delusion does even sort-of make sense at the highest levels of the enterprise, and at the very lowest, because in both cases there's just the one nucleus on the chart – at the top, nothing below than brawn; at the bottom, nothing above but management. But in the middle, the delusion falls apart: up, down, sideways, there has to be both 'brain' *and* 'brawn'. There, management is not and cannot be 'special and different': it's just one more service amongst many, and nothing more than that.

Breakdown of 'special and different' delusion in the middle layers

Something else that's easy to miss in the microscope – in fact very hard to see – is the process of communication and coordination that occurs both between the subsidiary services within the cell, and between the cell and other cells with which it's associated. To make sense of viable systems, we need to understand not just the visible services, but the more subtle web of connections between them.

Service-relationships

At this point we can drop the cell-analogy, and go straight to business. What we're mainly interested in here is the differences between *intra-service* relationships – those that occur within the service itself – and *inter-service* relationships that link between services, vertically, horizontally, and in other ways.

The main intra-service relationships are those between the 'brain' and 'brawn' – the subsidiary *delivery-services* that do the concrete work of the overall service unit. In classic business terms, there are requirements and definitions of 'critical success factors' (CSFs) going downward from 'brain' to brawn'; and performance-records – particularly the 'key performance indicators' (KPIs) – that go upward from 'brawn' to 'brain'.

> More precisely, they pass between the 'brain' of the service and the 'brain'-services *within* the subsidiary 'brawn' services – a point we'll come back to later.

The most visible inter-service relationships are those between the overall service and the 'customer' for the service – usually called the 'requester', in service-oriented architecture. The requirements for these relationships are typically documented in some form of 'service-level agreement' (SLA) or 'operational level agreement' (OLA), which should – but sometimes doesn't – also define the metrics by which the quality of service would be monitored. So if we view a typical business-function as a service, we would expect to see a structure something like this.

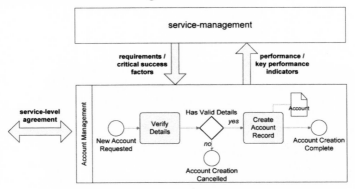

A simple example of business function as encapsulated service

That's probably all of the relationships that would be described in a typical IT-centric version of service-oriented architecture. In fact in most cases we'd be lucky to be presented with anything more than the basic 'brawn to brawn' service-to-service transactions, without any quality-of-service metrics at all – which is a serious problem in itself for IT service-management.

But in addition to those missing metrics, there are also other key inter-service relationships of which we need to keep track. Although there are others, as we'll see later, the most obvious of these are the extensions of the same intra-service relationships – requirements, CSFs, KPIs and so on – up and down the service-hierarchy tree. Requirements cascade downward; report-metrics cascade upward, much as described in Balanced Scorecard and the like.

Hierarchy of services, each with their own performance-measures

Each 'brawn' within the service is really a complete service in its own right, so to some extent those 'intra-service' relationships and messages are actually *inter*-service relationships between the 'brain' of the 'parent'-service and the 'brain' of the respective 'child'-service. *The 'brain' of the service is itself a service:* in most cases its main 'customers' are other 'brain'-services upstream and downstream in the service-hierarchy.

In addition to these, there are also a variety of 'horizontal' relationships that focus not just on individual transactions, but co-ordination of the full end-to-end processes in which the service takes part. And when we remember that in a real enterprise this will include *human* contexts as well as the machine-to-machine messages, we also need to include some other, often more subtle relationships and 'transactions' around auditing, monitoring, quality, and trust, that keep each service and the overall enterprise on track and 'on purpose'.

When we look at all the requirements of an enterprise, viewed in terms of the living-organism metaphor, we can see that *every* sub-unit in the enterprise would need to have some means to do all of the following:

- to *do* its task – in other words, deliver its services
- to *sense* and report on its perception of its internal and external environment
- to *remember*, using some kind of repository of knowledge about its past
- to *coordinate* its activities with other systems and services
- to *plan* its activities in some way, coordinating its strategies and tactics with others
- to *adapt* to and, where possible, improve its own environment and operation
- to maintain a sense of *purpose*, to contrast its present condition with a desired future condition

Every living system does all of this in some way: even an amoeba has a sense of purpose and direction, if only in terms of a simple reflex response to its chemical context. Every part of a functioning enterprise does all of this, too – because if it doesn't, or if it doesn't do it well, the enterprise won't survive. Which means that if we want to build a true architecture of the service-oriented enterprise, this is the true scope of what we have to be able to describe, and to model.

But if this all seems a lot to include in a service-oriented architecture, don't worry. The principles, and even the practice, have all been well-documented for decades, in the formal discipline of management cybernetics, 'the science of effective organisation'. And for this we can turn to *the* fundamental tool in that field: Stafford Beer's 'Viable System Model'.

Services as viable systems

A *viable system* is any organised system that combines, and resolves to its benefit, all of the 'survival demands' in a changing environment. In business terms, that means an enterprise that not only survives change, but *thrives* on it; for a service-oriented architecture, that implies a structure that is not only capable of mon-

36

itoring its environment, and any changes in that environment, but also *self*-adapting to change wherever practicable.

So the Viable System Model (VSM) describes the fundamental structure and organisation of any viable system. In essence, it's a service-oriented architecture, in much the same sense as in the previous section.

> We won't need to go into the full detail of the VSM here – for that, see Stafford Beer's book *The Brain of the Firm*, or Patrick Hoverstadt's excellent *The Fractal Organization*. One of the model's most important characteristics, though, is its recursive structure: the same basic pattern repeats at every level of the enterprise. As a result, it has extraordinary *scalability*: it has been used for every type and size of organisation, from small co-operatives in Britain, and mid-sized factories in Spain, all the way up to the management of the entire economy of a country – Allende's Chile, way back in the early 1970s.
>
> Beer's 'Cybersyn' system for Allende not only created a true 'balanced scorecard' technique two decades before Balanced Scorecard, but showed how to use that information to make real-time decisions about the operations of a huge enterprise. (The system was destroyed by the military junta shortly after their assassination of Allende, not because it didn't work, but apparently because it had been *too* successful in creating resilience against the covert 'games' of the foreign companies that had bankrolled their coup...) The Chilean website which describes that project – see *Resources* below – is a real eye-opener about what can be achieved when even very limited resources are combined with a few truly innovative ideas. Many of those ideas will still seem advanced even by today's standards, several decades later. Go see for yourself: *very* strongly recommended for any enterprise architect or IT-architect.

The VSM was originally intended as a way to describe the actions and information-flows needed for management of the system – the metaphoric equivalent of a nervous-system for the 'viable enterprise', but not much more than that. So whilst it's a powerful model from an IT-architecture perspective, it does need some expansion to make it work well as a generic model for *all* types of 'viable services', rather than solely for 'viable IT-systems'. We'll explore that later: for now, the main point is that it starts from the same basic 'brain/brawn' split that we've seen earlier as a base to understand the structure of services.

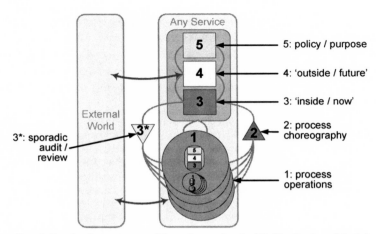

Specialised sub-systems with each service in Viable System Model

In the model, Beer represents these by a rectangle for 'brain' – the management-services – and a circle for 'brawn' – the delivery-services. Each 'brain' can manage any number of 'brawn' units – each of which in turn contains its own 'brain' and any number of subsidiary 'brawns'. Crucially, Beer splits the 'brain' into three distinct subsidiary functions, and includes two other functions which are, in part at least, *outside* of the 'brain/brawn' pair.

All these functions or 'systems' are assigned numbers, as follows:

- system-5: maintain *policy*, purpose and identity
- system-4: *research* and report on the external environment, and develop *strategy*
- system-3: *plan* and *manage* the operations activities
- system-3*: *monitor* and *verify* by sporadic audit of activities
- system-2: *regulate* and *coordinate* activities with other systems and services at a tactical level
- system-1: *do* the allotted task of the overall service, and sense and report on the internal environment

> In the original model, what is now labelled 'system-3*' was first considered to be part of the system-3 management tasks; but practical experience, such as with the Chilean 'Cybersyn' project, showed that it did need to be handled separately. As we'll see later, the VSM assignment for system-3*, as 'sporadic audit', is actually only one of a whole category of subsidiary 'pervasive services' with this relationship to the management-services.

A glance back at that list at the end of the previous section would show that the VSM 'systems' cover most of those requirements: the only items missing are the two about knowledge and memory, and adaptation and improvement. Although both of these are partly covered by the definition for system-4, they're actually better handled by an expansion of the roles of system-2 and system-3*.

Although the VSM itself focuses on management (the system-3, -4, -5 cluster) and the information-flows needed for management, the real tension of importance in the enterprise is between purpose (the single top-level system-5) and the expression of that purpose in practice (the multitude of system-1 entities). *Everything else – including management – is just a support-service towards that end.*

Without those support-services, the purpose won't happen: hence management does matter, and matter a lot. But we do need to keep a perspective here, and perhaps a better perspective even than the VSM itself: we need to give equal attention to *all* of the services and service-categories, at every level and of every type, and avoid any over-emphasis on just one or two at the expense of all the others.

In effect, every service, whatever its level in the service-hierarchy, has the same internal structure and relationships; yet each has its own specialist role within the organism or, at the enterprise scale, the superorganism. Each service has its set of subsidiary services or 'child-services' with four possible categories of functions:

- task-delivery or delivery-support (system-1) – see *Principles – Delivery services*, p.42
- service-management (system-3, system-4, system-5) – see *Principles – Management services*, p.49
- 'horizontal' coordination with other services (system-2) – see *Principles – Coordination services*, p.62
- functions to keep the overall service on track and aligned with enterprise purpose (system 3*) – see *Principles – Pervasive services*, p.71

Classic management texts would bundle everything other than task-delivery into the service-management services. But as the VSM diagram shows, coordination and audit *do* need to be addressed separately – not least because they need to operate under a different type of management-structure, and operate in a completely different way to the vertical hierarchy of the main service-management.

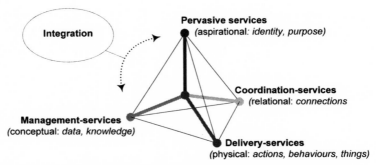

Service-functions and the tetradian architecture-dimensions

The four types of services also align with the four architecture-dimensions of the *tetradian* model described in other books in this series:

- delivery services: *physical* dimension – actions and transactions
- management services: *conceptual* dimension – information, planning and reporting
- coordination services: *relational* dimension – connections across between people and across the silos
- pervasive services: *aspirational* dimension – enterprise purpose, identity and values

We also need to explore how the different types of services communicate with each other – see *Principles – Properties and patterns*, p.78. In most cases these would pass through predefined 'normal channels' – though note that many of these, particularly with people-based services, could use a range of means that may be much broader than just the usual IT-type transactions, records and messages. But in some cases, an urgent message or other exception – what Beer describes as an 'algedonic' communication – will need to jump from *any* service to any other: and these must be able to bypass those 'normal channels' completely – whether middle-management like it or not! So whilst the VSM does describe all the information-channels needed by a complete viable-system, it's not always either the same or as simple as conventional IT-centric descriptions might expect.

For now, though, let's look at those service-function types in more detail – starting with the main task-delivery functions.

Application

- What structures would you identify in your existing enterprise? In what ways are these structures layered, repeating the same kind of structures at different hierarchical levels?
- In what ways are these structures divided between 'brain' and 'brawn'? Who or what sets the overall purpose for each structure?
- In what ways do these structures communicate with each other? Via what mechanisms? And for what purposes?
- How are the activities of the various services coordinated? At each level? Between levels? And as nodes within end-to-end processes?
- How would you identify the efficiency, reliability and overall effectiveness of any service? Of communication and coordination within and between services? How would you improve any of this? What support – or lack of it – do you gain from the structure itself in doing so?

Resources

📖 Balanced Scorecard: see Wikipedia summary at en.wikipedia.org/wiki/Balanced_scorecard

📖 Balanced Scorecard: see RS Kaplan and DP Norton, *Balanced Scorecard: Translating Strategy into Action* (Harvard Business School Press, 1996)

📖 Viable System Model: see Wikipedia summary at en.wikipedia.org/wiki/Viable_System_Model

📖 Cybersyn project, Chile, 1971-73: see www.cybersyn.cl/ingles/cybersyn/index.html

📖 Stafford Beer and the Viable System Model: see Stafford Beer, *Brain of the Firm* (Allen Lane: The Penguin Press, 1972)

📖 Viable System Model in organisation design: see Patrick Hoverstadt, *The Fractal Organization: Creating sustainable organizations with the Viable System Model* (Wiley, 2008)

📖 The 'tetradian' as architecture-dimensions: see chapter 'Dimensions of Architecture' in Tom Graves, *Real Enterprise Architecture: beyond IT to the whole enterprise* (Tetradian, 2008)

PRINCIPLES – DELIVERY SERVICES

Summary

The 'delivery' services are what are most likely to be understood *as* the services of the enterprise – the visible work done by the organisation's workforce and systems. In addition to those which deliver services or products to external customers, there are many which provide internal support in a multitudinous variety of forms. Some of these latter services may be outsourced – especially those 'non-core' services which provide only a kind of background or infrastructural support.

Details

> Technically speaking, every service is a 'delivery service', since by definition every service delivers something for some specified 'customer'. What we're talking about in this section, though, are those services which deliver something of value to the enterprise's external customers, either directly, or in direct support of that external-service delivery.
>
> Remember too that every service actually has the same structure; *every* service delivers something, manages itself, coordinates itself with others, and aligns to the overall values of the enterprise. In these sections we'll explore the effective emphases of each type of service – the roles they play within the enterprise and its purpose – but in terms of their *internal* structure they're all much the same. The specific implementations of each service may differ a lot, of course, but that's something else we'll look at later.

Description

In the service-oriented enterprise, service-delivery is what the enterprise *does*. Exactly what it delivers, and how it does so, will depend on the nature of the enterprise and on the layer of detail in scope; but it's always about some kind of action or transaction, something that is done.

The bulk of the enterprise is made up of delivery-services, in an often bewildering variety of forms and at a multitude of levels of detail and abstraction. A service may also be delivered by *any* appropriate combination of people, machines and IT, with the emphasis here on 'appropriateness to context' rather than on the outward form – a key point that IT-architects do sometimes tend to forget!

Delivery-services will typically be split into three categories:

- *external-delivery* to an end-customer of the enterprise
- *internal-delivery*, where the 'customer' is another service within the enterprise, and what is delivered is 'core' to the enterprise purpose
- *infrastructure* and other support-services that are 'non-core' to the enterprise purpose

There are no intrinsic distinctions between these categories, no *inherent* reason why any given type of service should always be placed in one category than another: the distinctions depend on context, not content. Building-maintenance or cleaning-services, for example, might be regarded as 'non-core' infrastructure by most organisations, but would be the 'core' external-delivery for a company that provided glazing services or cleaning-materials. So although – like the various organs in the human body – they may take different forms and have different functions in the enterprise, these are *all* 'delivery-services', and structurally should be treated in exactly the same way.

Viable system context

In viable-system terms, these are the *VSM system-1* services.

In VSM diagrams, these are represented by a circle, which also contains within itself the nested sets and subsets of its 'child' VSM systems.

In the tetradian architecture-model, these represent the *physical* dimension.

In the organism-metaphor, these might represent, for example, the muscles, tendons and sinews ('external delivery'), digestion and lungs ('internal delivery'), and vascular systems and skeleton ('infrastructure') of the enterprise. These also provide the real-world sensors that deliver sense-information for all subsequent decision-making.

Enterprise context

At the most abstract level of the enterprise – as shown by system-1 entities in the top-level VSM diagram – there would be at least one delivery-service, up to perhaps a maximum of seven. (In practice, anything more than around seven becomes too unwieldy to manage.) The number of top-level delivery-services is determined by the number of *distinct* customer-groups or markets that the enterprise will service – 'distinct' in the sense of fundamentally different needs and services, rather than simple market-categories such as age-group or geographic distributions – plus an arbitrary set of high-level internal support-services.

At board-level, these would typically be represented by the Chief Operations Officer (COO), and perhaps also by the Chief Technical Officer (CTO) in an IT-centric enterprise. Given the prominence of finance in most organisations, those support-services would probably also be represented at board-level, by the Chief Finance Office (CFO).

In the body of the enterprise, the delivery-services would be represented by explicit business-units and work-teams, often split on functional or geographic boundaries. The actual services would be delivered by any appropriate combination of people, machines and IT.

Sub-units or variants

From a VSM perspective, all delivery-services are equal: there are no sub-units or variants as such. But as described above, there in effect three sub-types, though the distinctions between them are often more about role and perception than any intrinsic difference. These distinctions would become more evident as we move downward in the detail-hierarchy.

External-delivery (value-chain)

At the higher levels, the 'external customer' for external-delivery services would literally be external, an 'outside' stakeholder. At the detail-levels, it's more often that the service is directly in-line within a value-chain: there is an *end-customer* for the overall value-chain, but the direct 'customer' for the delivery-service will often be the next service in line in the end-to-end business-process.

Each service should usually have a single defined 'customer' at the respective level of abstraction, though may itself be a customer of any number of suppliers.

There are an infinite variety of forms of delivery-service and service-content, each dependent on industry and context. A law-firm, for example, might deliver the following external services:

- legal advice

- court representation
- contract preparation and review
- conveyancing of commercial property

External-delivery services are invariably perceived as 'core' business functions: without them, the reason for the enterprise in its present form would cease to exist. As a result, they are usually described as 'profit-centres' in corporate accounts.

Internal delivery (support services)

The 'customer' for an internal-delivery service is another service internal to the enterprise: it will not have any direct contact with an external customer of the enterprise.

Each internal-delivery service will typically have only a small number of 'customers' at the respective level of abstraction – perhaps only one. It may itself be a customer of any number of suppliers.

Examples in the law-firm might include:
- library
- physical-records archive
- database, knowledge-base and information-systems

Internal-delivery services are usually perceived as 'core' business functions: in some cases the enterprise could perhaps obtain them from other service-providers, but would not be able to do so with high efficiency or effectiveness. As a result, although they are usually described as 'cost-centres' in corporate accounts, they are rarely available for outsourcing.

Infrastructure services

As for internal-delivery services, the 'customer' for an infrastructure service is another service internal to the enterprise. It will not have any direct contact with an external customer of the enterprise. It may in reality exist only in virtual form within the enterprise, in that it is actually delivered by an external service-provider – a 'supplier' to the enterprise.

Each infrastructure service will typically have many 'customers' at the respective level of abstraction. It may itself be a customer of any number of suppliers.

Examples in the law-firm might include:
- energy and other consumables
- building-management and maintenance

- logistics and mail-services
- provision of office-consumables
- recruiting, salary, benefits, expenses and other routine people-management
- training and certification

Infrastructure services are usually perceived as 'non-core' business functions: the enterprise could operate without them as internal services, or obtain them from other service-providers, without significant detrimental impact on business efficiency or effectiveness. Often such services, although essential, are regarded as a distraction from the main focus of the enterprise. As a result, they are usually described as 'cost-centres' in corporate accounts, and are often available for outsourcing.

Interfaces

Interfaces with service-customers (as *provider*) and suppliers (as *requester*) are all horizontal peer-to-peer relationships, at the same functional level. Each of these interfaces would be defined and monitored through a service-level or operations-level agreement, which may be either explicit – such as in a contract, or a message-format – or implicit in a trust-relationship such as the stereotypic 'gentlemen's agreement'.

Delivery-service interfaces

Secondary interfaces with other internal 'systems' would include:

- 'downward' from local management (system-3): schedules, priorities and other requirements
- 'upward' to local management: performance summaries, escalated exceptions
- 'upward' to local strategy (system-4): future-context information gleaned from service-delivery activities

46

- 'sideways' with local cross-silo coordination (system-2): inter-service schedules and other information-exchange for end-to-end processes
- 'sideways' with any level of representatives for pervasive-services (system-3*): auditing, monitoring and capability-development for alignment with enterprise values

Each delivery-service is an encapsulation of all of the subsidiary services needed to deliver the nominal service at that level of abstraction. Hence there are many implied interfaces 'downward' into the detail of the abstract service hierarchy, until eventually something real is delivered to a real customer or received from a real supplier.

Note that unlike the management information-flows and suchlike, which often *are* reflected in tangible reports and other entities at each level of abstraction, *the root-level transactions are the only real items of service-delivery*. Every other nominal 'service' above that root-level is an aggregation or abstraction for reporting purposes only, and does not exist as such in reality.

Application

- What services does your enterprise deliver as a whole? How would you identify and define the customers for those overall services?
- What distinctions and categorisations of customers start to appear as you move downward through the layers of abstraction, towards individual, explicit transactions?
- What are the 'core services' of the enterprise? What services are 'non-core'? By what means do you distinguish between 'core' and 'non-core'?
- If the corporate accounts use a categorisation of 'profit centres' versus 'cost centres', what characteristics are used to make such distinctions? What impact do such distinctions have on service-funding, on service-provision, on relationships between services, and on responsibilities for delivery or supply of those services?
- In what ways do you identify explicit delivery-services at each level of abstraction in the enterprise? How do the descriptions of and 'customers' for these services change as you move downwards towards the detail-layers of real service-delivery?

- Given a categorisation of 'external-delivery', 'internal-delivery' and 'infrastructure', how and why would you assign different delivery-services to each of those categories?
- What makes a service necessary to overall operation of the enterprise? What does each service deliver to the enterprise?
- What characteristics determine whether or not a given service is suitable for outsourcing, or purchase from an external service-provider?

Resources

📖 Stafford Beer and the Viable System Model: see Stafford Beer, *Brain of the Firm* (Allen Lane: The Penguin Press, 1972)

📖 Viable System Model in organisation design: see Patrick Hoverstadt, *The Fractal Organization: Creating sustainable organizations with the Viable System Model* (Wiley, 2008)

PRINCIPLES – MANAGEMENT SERVICES

Summary

The management services focus on information-flows and on the future of the enterprise. As such, they represent the 'brain of the firm' – though for that reason may perhaps gain an excess amount of attention compared to the needs or natures of other service-types. Their interfaces tend naturally towards hierarchies and silo-structures, creating a risk of the 'Taylorist trap' of over-escalated issues, and sometimes serious difficulties in coordination of end-to-end processes. These can be resolved by treating management not as 'special and different', but as just another set of services within the overall enterprise.

Details

Description

In the service-oriented enterprise, management is about what the enterprise *knows*, how it *thinks*, and how it *decides*. Although the details will differ with each enterprise, there is actually very little difference in overall function or content or even in structure – hence one reason why managers may move from one enterprise to the next with relative ease, and relative success.

> There's a subtle trap here that has killed many a company, and is very difficult to spot if you've been trained only in the Taylorist tradition of 'scientific management'. This is that whilst the management skills themselves may be portable, the information-content for management is much the same everywhere, *that which is managed is not the same* – it's different with every context.
>
> Taylorism assumes that the 'brain' always knows best; and the higher up you are in the hierarchy, the more knowledge you're presumed to have. Hence the 'higher-ups' are assigned more authority, and more decision-making responsibility. So whenever there's a problem, an exception to the predefined work-instructions in The Book, it's 'escalated' upward in hierarchy for decision; and 'actions' passed back down again from on high as to what to do to resolve the problem.

But the catch is that this only works when the problem is one of conceptual knowledge. Often the real need is not 'thinking with the head' – the theory – but what we might call 'thinking with the hands' – which can only be gained through skills, through what may well be years of hard-won hands-on practical experience. Yet the Taylorist principles give preference and precedence to people who are strong on abstractions and strong on theory – but give little or no credit for competence in the practice. Which means the 'decision-makers' are less and less likely to be competent to make *practical* decisions – a situation that gets *worse* with each step higher up the tree.

As Deming demonstrated, the proper place for practical decisions is at the point of practice: sometimes we need to 'escalate' *down* in the hierarchy, not up. But in Taylorism, the workers at each level are deemed to be 'brainless brawn', and have no power to make decisions. In effect, they have the nominal responsibility, but no authority. Instead, the authority is 'owned' by the manager: and if the managers insist on holding on to responsibilities for detail-concerns for which they don't have the practical competence, *everyone* is stuck.

The only way to get 'unstuck' is to recognise that 'higher' knowledge is not necessarily 'better' knowledge: what matters is whether it's the *appropriate* knowledge. And the only way we can find out what type of knowledge *is* appropriate in any given context is by creating a respectful partnership of peers. Management is just a service, just like any other in the enterprise: theory serves practice just as much as practice serves theory.

I saw this at work time and again in my years as a systems-analyst in aircraft research. Each year a new generation of bright young graduates would appear on the site, waving their shiny new engineering degrees, certain that they knew everything about aircraft design. And each year, with the full agreement of the foreman, the machinists and fitters would smile, and go into a subtle work-to-rule: they would do *exactly* what the new engineers asked – which meant that nothing worked. Components were made for assemblies that couldn't be assembled; materials mated that wouldn't last more than a matter of minutes in the field; all precisely as per the design-specification… Some of the young engineers took longer than others, perhaps, but they all learnt soon enough that there was another knowledge they needed here: a knowledge of how to make things work in the *real* world, rather than only the comfortable world of theory. If they wanted their designs to succeed in practice, they needed to respect that other knowledge, and work *with* it, no matter how different it was from their own.

Would have been good if some of the managers I've met in my time had learnt that lesson too. Oh well…

Management-services form natural hierarchies, with each level representing a different layer of abstraction. Enterprise-architects would be familiar with some of these, such as from the classic Zachman set, with its five, or six, or seven distinct layers, from unchanging 'universals' at the top to the real-time maelstrom of operations at the bottom. Real enterprises will provide many variations on that theme, such as further splits on boundaries of geography or market or function, but the base-principle of a layered hierarchy of abstraction will remain the same.

Echoing the same layering, the Viable System Model embeds three distinct – and functionally different – layers within the 'brain' of each system-1 delivery-service:

- *policy* – purpose, identity, imperatives, vision and values
- *strategy* – 'outside / future'
- *direction* – 'inside / now'

The different functions of these subsystems also align to different abstractions of *time*, from far future all the way through to near past. Note, though, that these apply in their own ways within *every* system and service – not just at the top of the enterprise management hierarchy.

Viable system context

In viable-system terms, these are the **VSM system-3, system-4** and **system-5** services.

In VSM diagrams, these are represented by a rectangle for the management-services collective set, containing three squares or rectangles for the three sub-systems, with system-5 uppermost.

In the tetradian architecture-model, these represent the *conceptual* dimension; system-5 also represents the management expression of the *aspirational* dimension.

In the organism-metaphor, these represent the brain and nervous-system of the enterprise – action-requests going out to the whole enterprise, and sense-information returning back, with decision-making taking place both centrally and distributed throughout the enterprise.

Enterprise context

At the most abstract level of the enterprise – as shown by the bounding rectangle around the system-3, -4 and -5 entities in the top-level VSM diagram – there will be exactly one overall management service.

At board-level, the system-5 ('policy') should be represented by the Chief Executive Officer (CEO) or Managing Director (MD). The system-4 ('strategy') would typically be represented by the whole board, with CEO or MD as chair; or perhaps ideally by an explicit role of Chief Strategy Officer (CSO). The system-3 ('direction') would typically be represented by the MD or COO.

In the body of the enterprise, the management-services would be represented by distinct groups or individuals with the respective assigned roles. For example, a formal strategy-group may take on responsibility for the system-4 'strategy' services directly below board-level; various staff-members will take on the system-3 'direction' role – often with a job-title of 'manager' – at most levels within the enterprise. Further down in the hierarchy-tree, the respective tasks may well form only a part of the responsibilities of a work-role – especially for the system-4 'strategy' and system-5 'policy' tasks.

Sub-units or variants

In the VSM, as described above, there are three distinct services that combine to make up the overall management-service within each system-1 unit: system-5 'policy', system-4 'strategy' and system-3 'direction'.

> Whilst working on this chapter, I came across a point about the VSM that I hadn't noted before, and which may be important for anyone applying systems-theory principles in enterprise-architecture.
>
> I base much of my own enterprise-architecture work on a rethink of Tuckman's well-known five-phase 'Group Dynamics' project-lifecycle, as an overview-model of the overall workings of an enterprise:
>
> – *forming*: purpose, identity, strategy; also far-future
>
> – *storming*: people-issues; anywhere from far-future to far-past
>
> – *norming*: plans and schedules; also near-future
>
> – *performing*: production; also '*now!*'
>
> – *adjourning* (or *mourning*): completions; also near- to mid-past
>
> Yet when we look at the 'management' section of the VSM, it seems it covers only three of the five Group Dynamics phases: VSM system-5 'policy' aligns to 'forming'; system-4 'strategy' aligns to the later part of 'forming', plus most of 'norming'; and system-3 'direction' aligns to the later part of 'norming', plus most of 'performing'.
>
> But there's no explicit VSM coverage at all of the 'storming' phase, the people-issues – which seems strange considering Beer's own strong personal bent towards 'left-ish' participatory politics. And although the original VSM system-3*', 'random-audit', does sort-of touch the 'adjourning' phase, it only does so on an occasional basis – not the continuous processes needed for completions and lessons-learned.
>
> This gap may stem from the VSM's history as a model of information-flows for management and the like; but it still seems a huge hole in the

> coverage of what's actually needed for systemic design of management processes. Odd...
>
> We do cover these 'missing' issues here, via our extended system-2 as 'coordination services' and system-3* as 'pervasive services'. But if we use only the original VSM to describe management-services, we'll need some alternate means to cover those missing issues – or we'll once again end up with intractable issues that we can't see.

Management-services at any level should always include exactly one of each of the following subsidiary services.

Policy, purpose, identity

The VSM system-5 'policy' service is responsible for 'holding the vision' for the enterprise: anything to do with principles, policy, values, identity and so on. Ultimately, it's also responsible for compliance to regulation and legislation, and defining how such should be interpreted in the enterprise – and that includes the more subtle 'regulations' of the social milieu or 'corporate culture' in which the enterprise operates.

At the topmost level, the 'policy' service sets the anchor – or perhaps 'guiding star' – for the entire enterprise:

Purpose defines the enterprise priorities

Within each layer – each 'system-1' instance – it's the role of the local 'policy' service to interpret those priorities, and to assess and evaluate all activities in terms of those priorities. The function here is the enterprise's means to handle uncertainty: whenever we encounter a real-world context in which the usual rules don't apply, and analysis is either too misleading or too slow, the principles and purpose define the priorities to guide those decisions we need to make. Purpose *matters*.

But here we hit up against a nasty problem: there's almost always a difference between the principles and values that the enterprise would espouse in public, and the often unconscious ones used in its actual decision-making. And sometimes that difference can be *huge* – so huge that no-one in the enterprise can see it, or *dare* see it. Under those circumstances, what we'll need most is some perhaps-painful honesty, for which one useful guide is Stafford Beer's oft-quoted acronym POSIWID:

"The purpose of a system is what it does"

If we don't like what the system does, or if what it's doing doesn't align to the espoused values, we need to look closer at how we're managing purpose in the enterprise. The *actual* 'purpose' of the system is what it does: not just what we hope or believe or would like to pretend it does. If we say that safety is a high priority, yet we have a high accident-rate, what we've built is a system in which safety is actually a low priority: the problem is *systemic*, right at the core of the enterprise – and that misalignment is simply *reflected* in the work-practices, not caused by them.

To change that misalignment on safety – to use the same example – we would need to review *everything* in terms of safety: not just processes, but performance-metrics, work-incentives, knowledge-sharing and the rest. So *the metrics we need to run the business are defined by the business-purpose*: the priorities define the content that we need in the enterprise 'Balanced Scorecard'.

> Those metrics pass up and down the tree via the system-3 'direction' service – but to make sure that we can actually trust the figures and values reported in those metrics, and that they really do mean what they claim to mean, we need to verify as well, by some kind of audit. We also need to support the root-level practices, and any changes needed in those practices, that end up being reported in those metrics. More on both of those concerns when we look later at the 'pervasive services' – see *Principles – Pervasive services*, p.71.

In the same way, purpose also acts as the guide and final arbiter for decision-making in strategy (VSM system-4), in direction (VSM system-3), and in the balance between them. As we move further down the tree, this 'purpose' also includes constraints imposed by any applicable legislation and the like; and also any standards either chosen by the enterprise, or mandated or recommended by the market and milieu in which the enterprise operates – such as ISO-9000 certification for quality-systems, or an industry-specific XML-based messaging format. Purpose defines the standards – in every sense – by which the enterprise will measure itself.

Strategy ('outside / future')

The VSM 'system-4' service is responsible for assessing and inter-preting the milieu and market in which the enterprise operates, to enable the enterprise to respond *proactively* to its environment. Typical themes include:

- scanning the business environment for context and for signs of future change
- strategic foresight and forward planning, through tools such as scenario development and causal layered analysis
- assessment of strategic risk

54

- technical development, service development, product development and capability development

> Strategy is another whole field in itself – far more than we could cover here, given that the emphasis in this book is more on enterprise structure and architecture – so for now it's probably best just to leave it at that summary above. But there are plenty of good texts that do address those issues from an architecture-like perspective: see the *Resources* section below for some examples.

Another key role of the 'strategy' service is its engagement in 'strategic conversations' between past and future for the enterprise: for example, sales (past) versus marketing (future). Note, though, that this kind of 'conversation' needs to occur at *every* level of the enterprise, as appropriate to the respective context – and not solely in a separate 'strategy unit' that reports only to senior management.

Direction ('inside / now')

The VSM 'system-3' service is responsible for coordination of all the activities in this service's 'downstream' delivery-services – its collection of 'system-1' instances. In short, this is the classic role of middle-management: a myriad of day-to-day decision and detail. This is the most visible aspect of the overall management services, and usually accounts for the bulk of their work, too.

> In poorly-designed organisations, 'direction' is often the only part of the management-services that exists lower down in the hierarchy-tree – which literally leaves the organisation with only half a brain at those levels, capable only of dealing with the present and nothing else. *Not a good idea...*

In addition to directions to the 'child' delivery-services, the two main tasks here are *resource management,* going downward, and *performance management,* coming back up the tree. Balancing the conflicts within and between these two tasks is rarely easy.

Resource-management sounds simple enough until we remember that those resources have to come from somewhere first: and then it's suddenly not so simple... As we'll see later in the discussion on coordination-services, there's another Taylorist trap that hits overly-hierarchical organisations, because many of the resources have to come from *other* silos: and if we don't have good *horizontal* 'silo-busting' links, we'll be stuck with an unwieldy bureaucratic mess. Which is no-one's idea of fun – and far from effective, too.

The other catch is that to know what resources we need for the 'child' services, and how to divide the resources between them, we not only have to be clear about what we're asking them to deliver, but also how we measure what they've delivered – in other words, the performance-metrics. If we get the design of the performance-metrics wrong, or if they don't actually mean what they claim to mean, we'll again be stuck.

> It gets even more complicated when – as is usually the case – there are delays in the system, because the performance measures will always be somewhat out of sync with the timing of the resource-allocation. By the time these constraints echo across even a simple supply-chain – such as the four-partner chain in the classic Beer Game simulation – it takes a great deal of skill, experience *and mutual trust* to avoid an inefficient, ineffective, wasteful, frustrating, blame-filled mess. There are a fair number of online implementations of the Beer Game, so it's well worth having ago at it yourself: it's *not* easy.
>
> The Game was originally developed by Peter Senge and his colleagues at Sloan School of Management, from the 1960s onwards, as is explained in more detail in Senge's book on systems-theory, *The Fifth Discipline*. Both strongly recommended, anyway.

Yet another complication occurs with aggregation. In this section of the management-services, part of our task is to take all of the performance-metrics from the 'child'-services, and aggregate them into a single set of metrics to pass upward in the tree. The catch here is that we need to ensure that the same definitions and trans- forms are used in each of the 'children', otherwise we can no longer compare like with like, and the metrics risk being meaning- less. The same applies further up the hierarchy-tree, particularly when we have to compare metrics from different silos. Once again, there's plenty of room for confusion here...

> I came across a spectacular example of this in my work with a government department, when ministers and opposition almost came to blows over conflicting performance-figures that were supposedly derived from the same reporting-systems. They weren't, but the fact that all the files and data-fields had exactly the same names did kind of add to the confusion!
>
> I've described this incident in other books in this series, so I won't expand on it here: suffice it to say that this is where abstract-sounding notions such as 'database of record' and 'single source of truth' start to make real sense to the business-folks... More detail on this later when we look at 'business systems' – see the section 'Services and business- systems' in *Practice – The knowledge of services*, p.113.

And there is one more potential Taylorist trap of which we need to be aware: the tendency of managers to subsume all control of the coordination-services, and even the pervasive-services, into their own role. In part this is because classic 'scientific management' barely even acknowledges the need for such services; in part this is because rigid silo-structures often lead to a 'need' to control and limit any 'horizontal' connections, even though they're essential for any cross-silo end-to-end processes; and in part it's because, if there's no explicit support or resourcing for such services, the 'direction' management-service is probably the only place they can go, whether they fit there or not. But placing them there does cause all manner of intractable problems: more on those later in the respective sections, *Principles – Coordination services*, p.62, and *Principles – Pervasive services*, p.71.

Overall interaction

The overall management-service is delivered by the combined actions and interactions of the embedded system-3, system-4 and system-5.

Management services: internal interfaces

System-3 'direction' and system-4 'strategy' need to engage in continual 'strategic conversation' on a variety of themes such as:

- present sales ↔ future marketing
- present staff ↔ future needs
- present funding / resources ↔ future needs
- present products and production ↔ future needs

System-5 'policy' acts as the arbiter in this conversation, and also guides decision-making within each of the other two services. There would be some feedback into 'policy' from both, but the main drivers to policy-change will tend to occur more from higher up in the hierarchy-tree.

Interfaces

Management-services have symmetrical *vertical* connections, as both *provider* and *requester*, with the matching service-type above and below in the hierarchy-tree: system-5 'policy' connects to the 'policy' management-services in the 'parent' above and within the 'child' system-1 delivery-services below; and likewise for system-4 'strategy' and system-3 'direction'.

At the top of the tree – in other words the executive-management level – the 'upward' connections link to the operating milieu and business-environment. Policy comes 'down' in the form of legislation, regulation, standards and social expectations; reporting goes 'up', such as in the classic example of the company Annual Report.

Management services: interfaces with other systems

Descending downward, the hierarchy-tree terminates wherever management finally connects with actual service-delivery. In those cases, 'policy', 'strategy' and 'direction' do not connect with a matching counterpart, but with the service-delivery itself.

> This is also the effective source of the key distinctions between 'staff-management', 'middle-management' and 'line-management'.
>
> 'Staff' are at the top of the hierarchy-tree: they connect to other management-services below, but must deal with the real-world business-milieu above.
>
> Line-managers report to other managers upward, but they connect with *service-delivery* below – the horizontal links through which the 'real-world' work actually happens.
>
> Yet middle-managers are literally in the middle: they connect primarily with other managers both above and below.

> So there's a subtle danger here that middle-managers need never see anything other than the abstract, vertically-oriented world of management-services – an unfortunate trait whose disastrous consequences can be seen all too clearly in many organisations…

Because all of the primary connections are vertical, management-services have a tendency to form into hierarchies and silos. This is a natural *and necessary* consequence of these interfaces: the only key point to bear in mind is that the hierarchies are not the whole of the story.

The management-services also have secondary *horizontal* interfaces with coordination-services and pervasive-services. These interfaces are described in more detail in the respective sections – see *Principles – Coordination services*, p.62 and *Principles – Pervasive services*, p.71.

Application

- What management services exist in your enterprise? How would you distinguish between the different types of services at different layers of the enterprise?

- What happens to your perception of management in general when you choose to view them as *services*, rather than as mechanisms of control? What happens when you view each not as 'a thing apart', something inherently 'special and different' – as in the Taylorist machine-metaphor – but as just another type of service delivered to the enterprise?

- By what means are the system-5 services – purpose, policy and identity – defined in your enterprise? In what ways – if at all – is that process of definition distributed throughout the enterprise?

- In what ways and by what means are the *expression* of policy and identity distributed through the enterprise? Would you be able to use the term 'celebrated' to describe that policy and purpose, or does it seem more that it's something *imposed* on the rest of the enterprise by senior management? If the latter, what impact does this have on the enterprise as a whole? What, if necessary, could or should you do to change this?

- By what means are the system-4 services – business-intelligence, strategy, market-knowledge and the like – defined and determined in your enterprise? In what ways – if at all – are those processes distributed throughout the enterprise, or are those responsibilities and capabilities reserved to a specific team somewhere near the senior-management levels?

- In what ways and by what means are the *expression* of strategy and the like distributed through the enterprise? Is it co-developed, 'owned' throughout the enterprise, or does it seem more that it's something *imposed* on the rest of the enterprise by senior management? If the latter, what impact does this have on the enterprise as a whole? What, if necessary, could or should you do to change this?

- What detail-level tactics are used for direction and management of the 'downstream' delivery-services? What requirements and criteria are passed down the tree? In what forms? How are the requisite resources identified, obtained and distributed? What performance-metrics are passed back up from the downstream services? In what forms? How is the balance between requirements, resources and performance identified, verified and maintained? And in what ways, and by what transforms, are those performance-metrics aggregated to pass up the tree?

- How are the competing demands and priorities of policy, strategy and tactics resolved within the management-services? How does this vary at different levels and in different areas of the enterprise?

- What differences can you see between the espoused values and priorities of the enterprise, and the priorities which actually apply in practice? If "the purpose of the system is what it does", what is the *actual* 'purpose' of the enterprise? In what ways does this vary at different levels and in different silos of the enterprise? What could you do, in architecture terms, to bring the espoused purpose and actual purpose into closer alignment?

- If management-services tend naturally to form hierarchies and silos, because of the nature of their interfaces and interdependencies, what advantages and disadvantages to the enterprise as a whole can you see arising from this fact? What could you do to address the disadvantages without impacting the advantages?

Resources

📖 Stafford Beer and the Viable System Model: see Stafford Beer, *Brain of the Firm* (Allen Lane: The Penguin Press, 1972)

📖 Viable System Model in organisation design: see Patrick Hoverstadt, *The Fractal Organization: Creating sustainable organizations with the Viable System Model* (Wiley, 2008)

📖 Zachman-style layering of abstraction: see chapter 'Framework – layers' in Tom Graves, *Bridging the Silos: enterprise architecture for IT-architects* (Tetradian, 2008)

📖 Tuckman 'Group Dynamics' as project lifecycle and as organisation-model: see chapter 'An overview' (and overall book-structure) in Tom Graves, *Real Enterprise Architecture: beyond IT to the whole enterprise* (Tetradian, 2008)

📖 Relationship between enterprise-architecture and strategy: see Jeanne W. Ross, Peter Weill and David Robertson, *Enterprise Architecture As Strategy: Creating a Foundation for Business Execution* (Harvard Business Press, 2008)

🕸 Environmental scanning for business context: see Wikipedia summary at en.wikipedia.org/wiki/Environmental_scanning

🕸 Causal Layered Analysis: see www.metafuture.org/Articles/CausalLayeredAnalysis.htm

📖 Causal Layered Analysis: see Sohail Inayatullah [ed.], *The Causal Layered Analysis (CLA) Reader: theory and case studies of an integrative and transformative methodology* (Taipei: Tamkang University Press, 2004)

📖 Scenarios and 'strategic conversation': see Kees van der Heijden, *Scenarios: the art of strategic conversation* (Wiley, 2004)

🕸 Online implementation of the Beer Game: see www.masystem.com/beergame

📖 Business-oriented introduction to systems-thinking: see Peter Senge, *The Fifth Discipline: The Art & Practice of the Learning Organization* (Doubleday, 1990)

🕸 Online resources on 'Fifth Discipline': see www.fieldbook.com

PRINCIPLES – COORDINATION SERVICES

Summary

Where management-services build vertical hierarchies and silos within the enterprise, the 'coordination' services bridge *across* the silos, creating links for end-to-end processes, and enabling cross-functional integration. The services typically provide coordination in three distinct yet related areas: the routine running of business processes; changes to the business structure and capabilities; and changes to the overall purpose and direction of the business. The enterprise cannot operate without such services, though few will be formally recognised in management structures – an issue which itself can have serious impacts on enterprise effectiveness.

Details

Description

In the service-oriented enterprise, coordination-services create and maintain relationships across the enterprise. Without them, the enterprise would literally fall apart, as there would be nothing to hold the various functional silos together as an integrated whole.

Coordination-services provide horizontal links that bridge the gaps – or chasms – between the silos. Although always founded in relationships of some kind, some kind of cross-link *between* one thing or function or person and the next, the focus is also on what the enterprise *does* or *knows* – in contrast to the pervasive-services, which focus more on what the enterprise *is*.

> The enterprise cannot function effectively without the coordination-services: they're the functional glue that holds everything together. But yet again we hit a Taylorist trap here, because middle-managers often *hate* them, and hate them with a passion…
>
> Coordination-services are horizontal, which immediately is anathema to the vertical orientation of the management-services. By definition, they operate *between* silos, and hence seem to be outside of any ordinary manager's control. By insisting on cross-functional effectiveness over local efficiency, generalists may disrupt individual

managers' personal performance-targets – which can hit hard on performance-based bonuses. And almost all performance-metrics are both vertical and function-specific, which means that the more the cross-functional generalists do their real work, the less they appear to do. Often the only way to measure generalists' performance is at the level of the whole – hence that authority would have to pass right up the hierarchy, far 'above' where the generalists themselves might work, reinforcing the managers' grievances against apparent 'insubordination'. So overall, the managers' hatred is often understandable, even if not actually appropriate: but it's not a happy mix...

There *are* a few coordination-services that have formally-recognised business roles: the Programme Management Office is one such example. But most generalists I know hide behind blurry job-titles such as 'communications officer' or 'ideation manager', or operate as a 'skunk-works' under the shelter of a powerful patron. Yet it's a risky tactic: when the patron goes, so does the protection, and as one sardonic senior colleague put it, "if you're not being fired at least once every couple of years, you're probably not doing your job properly!"

A better solution is to break out of the Taylorist trap by showing that the problem comes from Taylorism itself – its absurd assumption that the vertical orientation of management alone is what makes the enterprise work. Yes, those vertical management-services do matter: but we need a better *balance* between vertical and horizontal. And we can create that by showing that the coordination-services do exist – and *need* to exist – and also what they actually *do* as the enterprise 'glue-logic'. We need real job-titles for cross-functional generalists; proper recognition for their roles at every level of the enterprise; and real *horizontal* performance-metrics for them,. too. A proper balance between local efficiency and overall effectiveness in managers' performance-based bonuses would also help, because that might take some of the heat – and hurt – out of the argument. We hope, anyway.

Note that for our purposes here, for enterprise-architecture, the *form* that the service takes is less important than that it exists, and that such coordination takes place at all. For example, typical people-roles might include:

- cross-functional bodies such as Programme Management Office
- troubleshooters and multi-skilled maintenance-crews
- individual cross-functional generalists
- 'linkers' and 'fixers' for end-to-end processes
- 'supernodes' in enterprise social-networks

Coordination may also occur through knowledge-sharing tools and techniques – some formal, some informal – such as:

- inter-service schedule-meetings and scheduling-systems

- shared standards
- shared glossary and thesaurus
- conferences and cross-functional meetings
- wikis, emails and social-network software
- online and offline collaboration tools

The services will typically take on one of three distinct roles, each aligned to one of the three types of management-services:

- *'Develop the Business'* – aligns with 'policy', VSM system-5
- *'Change the Business'* – aligns with 'strategy', VSM system-4
- *'Run the Business'* – aligns with 'direction', VSM system-3

Although the business-roles may differ, the overall structure and function of each type is the same in each case.

Viable system context

In viable-system terms, these are the **VSM system-2** services.

In VSM diagrams, these are represented by an upward-pointing triangle.

In the tetradian architecture-model, these represent the *relational* dimension, often intersecting with the *conceptual* dimension as the sharing of personal tacit knowledge or narrative knowledge.

In the organism-metaphor, these represent the 'superorganism' emergent-communication mechanisms for the enterprise – not yet fully understood in current biological sciences, but known to exist, for example, in insect social-systems such as beehives and ant-nests, and in polymorphic entities such as slime-moulds.

Enterprise context

In top-level VSM diagrams, coordination-services would usually be represented by a single system-2 triangle connected to the main management-services rectangle, although sometimes this may be split into separate system-2 instances for each of the three distinct management-services types.

At board-level, 'develop the business' coordination would always be represented by the CEO or MD; coordination for 'change the business' would typically also be represented by the CEO or MD, or sometimes by an explicit role of Chief Strategy Officer or Chief Change Officer; whilst 'run the business' coordination would be represented by the COO, or even – if usually inappropriately – by the CFO.

In the body of the enterprise, 'develop the business' coordination will typically occur in the uppermost levels of the hierarchy-tree as interpersonal and inter-group relationships, and as cross-functional events or 'suggestion box'-style tools and techniques rather than by explicit roles. 'Change the business' coordination typically takes the form of projects and project-teams, and more broadly by a dedicated Programme Management Office or equivalent. 'Run the business' coordination will be represented by a few explicit roles, probably supplemented by more covert roles and by shared responsibilities and personal connections across the silos.

Sub-units or variants

As described above, coordination-services have three variations in role: 'develop the business', 'change the business' and 'run the business'. Despite the differences in role, all three have essentially the same internal function and structure.

Develop the Business

This assists in the development and dissemination of policy, requirements and imperatives, and enterprise vision, values and identity – anything to do with the nature of the business and the principles that guide development and change. To do this, these services connect with the 'conversation' between the management services 'policy' and 'strategy' (VSM system-5 and system-4).

Typical examples include:

- business architecture and whole-of-enterprise architecture
- cross-functional policy and standards committees
- policy-development events – particularly 'large-group interventions' such as Future Search and Open Space

There's also some intersection here with the role of the pervasive-services, but it's important to realise that they're not the same.

The key difference is one of direction or emphasis, illustrated by the respective symbols on VSM diagrams: the coordination-services triangle points up, the pervasive-services triangle points down. The 'develop the business' coordination-services help ideas about policy, identity and overall direction to 'bubble upward' from anywhere in the enterprise, whereas pervasive-services are more about working downward to develop awareness of the *practical* implications of enterprise values, and capabilities to support and validate alignment with those values.

More on that in the next chapter – see *Principles – Pervasive services*, p.71.

Middle-managers may well regard these services as irrelevant to their operations, "just stuff for head-office idiots" and so on. Don't be surprised if you hear sarcastic comments about 'time-wasting nuisances' and the like, or throwaway remarks that "some people have *real* work to do, y'know?" Some of these may conceal subtle fears about threats to managers' authority, about bypassing 'the proper channels': such fears are understandable, and *do* need to be respected, if perhaps carefully *not* acknowledged in public...

The point is that, whether middle-managers like it or not, these processes do need to happen at *every* level of the enterprise. If they don't, there's no way to access the detail-level knowledge that arises from cross-functional interactions at the point of delivery and above – which would lead us straight back to the Taylorist trap again. We also risk losing people's engagement in the identity and purpose of the enterprise – and that engagement is something that is literally vital to the long-term viability of the enterprise.

One of our tasks as enterprise-architects, then, is to ensure that any systems we develop to support this will be available *every-where* in the enterprise – and that senior management mandate and authorise the systems' use by everyone, too.

Change the Business

This assists with coordination between the various stakeholders in any cross-functional change-project – a new capability, a changed business-process or whatever. To do this, it connects with the 'conversation' between the management services 'strategy' and 'direction' (VSM system-4 and system-3) in the respective service-delivery layers.

Typical examples include:

- project office and programme management office
- process-architecture, IT-architecture and other domain-architectures
- project teams and business-transformation teams
- capability-development teams
- training and skills-development

> As enterprise architects, we'll probably have least problems with middle-managers over this category of coordination-services, compared to the other two. Given the way it disrupts the steady-state assumptions of existing processes, change-management may be viewed as something of an evil, but at least as an unavoidable and possible even necessary evil!

Run the Business

This connects with the vertical communications 'down' and 'up' between the 'direction' management service (VSM system-3) and its 'child' delivery-services (VSM system-1), to guide coordination between delivery-services for end-to-end business-processes.

Typical examples include:

- inter-silo scheduling systems
- whole-of-process dashboards and process-flow models
- real-time critical-path analysis
- troubleshooters with formal authority to bridge silos
- knowledge-sharing systems such as wikis, best-practice reference-systems, 'problem boards'

Most of these services will be people-based or IT-based, or some combination of the two, but a few may be entirely mechanical. A classic example of the latter is the old 'token'-based safety inter-lock for single-line operation of a railway, which still has its counterparts in modern manufacturing.

The main work of these services is *inter*-silo, to facilitate end-to-end processes. Coordination *within* a silo is usually the role and responsibility of the 'direction' management-service (system-3), though these services may also provide feedback to management on inter-service scheduling and conflicts between those respective 'child'-services.

> Note, though, that this implied dual-responsibility for coordination of 'child'-services provides plenty of opportunity for clashes and conflicts between the vertically-oriented managers and the horizontally-oriented end-to-end link-roles. Such clashes occur often in organisational cultures that place an over-emphasis on managers' need to be 'in control' at all times. In such cases, proceed with caution – because if we're not careful, Here Be Dragons, breathing fire and fury!
>
> Making that link-function explicit will help; likewise emphasising that it's just feedback, helping to keep everything on track at a whole-of-enterprise level, not criticism or attack about 'failure to control'. But for the enterprise architect, care is the watchword here – that, and respect for the real difficulties faced by each side in this equation.

Interfaces

Coordination-services have symmetrical *horizontal* connections, as both **provider** and **requester**, to each of their 'customer' delivery-services for which they provide coordination. These connections may be modelled either as information-flows coordinating traffic and activities between the 'customer' delivery-services, or as the interface itself between those delivery-services.

As described above, these connections will link to each 'customer' as follows:

- 'develop the business': bridge between 'policy' and 'strategy' management-services
- 'change the business': bridge between 'strategy' and 'direction' management-services
- 'run the business': bridge between 'direction' management-service and any or all of its 'child' delivery-services

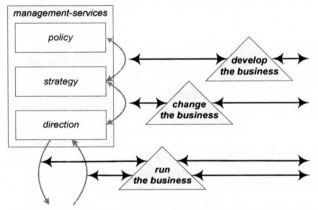

Coordination services: interfaces with other systems

Coordination-services will also have a symmetric pair of *vertical* connections, similar to those for the management-service set, linking 'upward' to an appropriate point in the overall management-hierarchy, such as:

- 'develop the business': sometimes further up the same branch, more often an almost direct link to a separate sub-branch high up in the tree
- 'change the business': usually a link to the matching next level up in a parallel branch dedicated to business change, such as a Programme Management Office programme-to-project-to-task management-hierarchy
- 'run the business': usually a link to the next level up in the same branch of the hierarchy-tree

The VSM specification shows the system-2 coordination-service only as an upward connection to its system-3 management-service and sideways to some or all of that service's 'child' system-1 delivery-services. Some VSM variants label this as 'regulation and tactical planning', though other terms are sometimes used. In effect this is a 'run the business' coordination, but one in which the link is more *within* a single silo – a special-case, in contrast to the more generic usage for the three distinct coordination-service roles, and for intra-silo *and* inter-silo integration.

Application

- What coordination-services exist within your enterprise? What forms do they take? What 'glue-logic' functions do they perform within the enterprise?

- Which – if any – of the coordination-services are formally recognised within the enterprise structure? For those services which do not have such recognition, how do they operate? From where do they obtain their resources?

- What performance-metrics are applied to coordination-services? If there are any, what weighting is assigned to local versus global or whole-of-enterprise effectiveness, in that assessment of personal or team performance?

- What clashes – if any – exist between management-services and coordination-services? If such clashes occur, what forms do they take, and which side tends to 'win' each argument? Who – and at what level – has the authority to act as arbiter in such clashes? And what are the consequences of any such clash?

- What distinctions do you see between coordination-services for 'Run the Business', 'Change the Business' and 'Develop the Business'? What different forms do they take? Are some of these represented only at specific levels of the enterprise? What changes – if any – would be needed to ensure that they are represented at every level of the enterprise?

- As an enterprise-architect, how would you represent such cross-functional services in process-models, service-models and function-models for the enterprise? How would you map the information-needs and process-flows for such services?

Resources

Stafford Beer and the Viable System Model: see Stafford Beer, *Brain of the Firm* (Allen Lane: The Penguin Press, 1972)

📖 Viable System Model in organisation design: see Patrick Hoverstadt, *The Fractal Organization: Creating sustainable organizations with the Viable System Model* (Wiley, 2008)

📖 Supporting generalists within the enterprise: see chapter 'The role of the generalist' in Tom Graves, *Real Enterprise Architecture: beyond IT to the whole enterprise* (Tetradian, 2008)

🕸 Large-group interventions: see Martin Leith's summary in www.largegroupinterventions.com/documents/leiths_guide_to_lgis.pdf

PRINCIPLES – PERVASIVE SERVICES

Summary

The pervasive services extend the enterprise imperatives from the topmost 'policy' management-service through to every part of the entire enterprise. One specific example, as described in the VSM, is sporadic audit, to verify reported results against actual activity. In practice, though, there would usually need to be a much broader range of equivalent pervasive-services, to 'audit' against other enterprise principles, policies and values – including themes such as safety, security, quality and corporate social-responsibility – and to create awareness of the issues, and the capabilities that are needed to support those themes throughout the enterprise.

Details

Description

In the service-oriented enterprise, the pervasive-services manage what the enterprise *is*. If, to quote Beer, the management-services represent 'the brain of the firm', the pervasive-services in a sense represent its heart or its soul.

> Once again we'd best take some care to avoid 'the religion bit' here! Some types of enterprise – particularly charities and not-for-profit organisations – might well use the term 'soul' in this context: but for most of us it's the principle behind that term that's more relevant. And the principle here is that of values and vision and policy and the like as the anchor or 'guiding star' for the enterprise, as described earlier (see p.53). Pervasive-services hold us to the anchor, or keep us on-track to that guiding-star: that's really all we're talking about here. If terms such as 'soul' are a problem, don't use 'em! – use whatever else works, as long as it does illustrate that key principle.

A service *serves* some purpose, something, someone: but what, or whom, does it serve? *How* does it serve? By what means does it ensure that it *does* serve? Such questions might perhaps sound somewhat abstract, but they're actually right at the core of service-orientation and the service-oriented enterprise.

71

To keep track on some purpose, there are three distinct aspects that we'll need:

- develop *awareness* that the purpose exists
- develop *capability* to serve that purpose
- *audit* to verify that we have indeed served that purpose

Somewhere in the middle we'll also need to *use* that capability so as to serve the purpose, but the other types of services – delivery, management and coordination – already handle those concerns. Here, with the pervasive-services, we're concerned with just those three sub-themes: awareness, capability and audit.

Some common business-examples of pervasive themes include:

- quality – including exception-handling, issue-tracking, corrective-action and process-improvement
- privacy, security and trust
- health, safety and environment
- ethics, social-responsibility and legal compliance
- cost-effectiveness and waste minimisation
- knowledge-sharing and innovation
- whole-of-enterprise efficiency and effectiveness

They're described as 'pervasive' themes because they need to pervade *every* part of the enterprise, to embed them into the core of every activity – in effect as a way of life, in the business sense. The pervasive-services need to exist in order to promulgate those themes throughout the enterprise: for example, simply stating that "such-and-such is an enterprise value" is not going to do anything useful at all – we need to *do* something to make it happen. People need to be told that these are the values; they need to know *why* those values exist, what purpose they serve, and so on. We need to create and maintain capabilities that will support those values – otherwise there's no *means* to support them. And performance-metrics need to be defined for every one of these themes – otherwise we can't audit them.

It sometimes needs a bit of sideways-thinking to do it, but we can also embed those values into processes, into software, into *every* activity.

To give a real example, one of our banking clients had a project to redesign the cash-management in their branches and ATMs. The aim was to reduce the bank's overall cash-holdings by ten percent – a non-trivial target, but achievable – in a way which would support enterprise values around effectiveness and financial performance, but also respect the skills and experience of individual staff.

> What they wanted was to achieve a better balance between central control – the 'big picture' view – and local knowledge – which warned about unusual ebbs and flow in cash-handling from fairs and markets and other local events. To tackle that, we created a forecasting system that garnered and combined all the different types of knowledge and event, giving appropriate weightings to each.
>
> We also needed to dissuade a common habit by bank-branches of ordering cash only at the last minute – which was not only expensive, but sometimes led to empty ATMs and even empty branches. So we changed the existing cash-order system to a much simpler 'today's to-do list', with all the essential activities already scheduled for the branches on their opening screen. The old over-used emergency-order process, which in the previous system was almost the first screen the bank-staff saw, did still exist – but the screen to access it was now three layers down. A simple, *practical* way to persuade people to change behaviours in line with purpose: not by bullying or cajoling, but by making it *easier* for them to do it right, and harder to do it wrong.

We can, and probably should, use the existing formal standards wherever practicable to guide the design and implementation of pervasive-services. Note, though, that these will each have their own emphases, covering different aspects of the issues: in quality-management, for example, ISO-9000 ensures that the capabilities exist in the enterprise, but Six Sigma ensures that they're *used*!

In principle we *can* operate the enterprise without any pervasive-services: but it certainly won't operate effectively, and probably won't operate for long, either. There needs to be an *explicit* purpose, an *explicit* vision and values, and a systematic means to manage legal compliance and the rest; because if we don't have these, what we get instead is POSIWID – the purpose of the system is what it does – and we probably won't like what it does at all… In that sense, the pervasive-services *matter*.

> We also need to beware of what we might call 'anti-services': concerns such as absenteeism, presenteeism, destructive rumour-mongering and so on. These invariably sabotage the intended purpose – if there is one – and will certainly damage enterprise effectiveness wherever they occur. Technically speaking they're not likely to be part of our responsibility as enterprise-architects, but there's plenty we can do to dissuade such happenings, as in the ATM example above. Do what we can, really.

Viable system context

In viable-system terms, these are the *VSM system-3** services – or rather, VSM system-3*, 'sporadic audit', is just one example of a much broader category of pervasive-services.

In VSM diagrams, these are represented by a downward-pointing triangle.

In the tetradian architecture-model, these represent the *aspirational* dimension.

In the organism-metaphor, these represent the distributed glandular communication systems – the endocrine-system hormones and suchlike – of the enterprise.

Enterprise context

It is probable that a top-level VSM diagram would aggregate all of the pervasive-services into a single system-3* entity, represented by a downward-pointing triangle linked to the system-5 'policy' management-service.

At board-level, all the pervasive-services should – nominally, at least – be represented by the CEO or MD, as the person formally responsible for defining and preserving enterprise identity and for promulgating all its policies, principles and values. In practice, some of those responsibilities may be taken on by other senior executives, such as the CFO for financial audit. Other examples might include the Chief Information Officer (CIO) or Chief Knowledge Officer (CKO) for knowledge sharing, or a possible Chief Security Officer for security-issues – the exact roles and requirements would vary from one enterprise to another.

In the body of the enterprise, the key responsibilities for development of awareness and capability for a pervasive theme would typically be assigned to a small team of 'evangelists', with the authority to act and interact with any part of the enterprise. Responsibilities for audit on that theme may be assigned either to the same team, or to a separate team: financial audit is one obvious example where such separation may be mandated by law. Overall, though, responsibilities for each pervasive theme are necessarily shared and owned by *everyone*: by definition, the theme must pervade *every* aspect of the entire enterprise.

This shared-responsibility applies not only within the bounds of the organisation, but extends also to all parts of the shared enterprise which are outside its bounds. For example, concerns about quality or security will *necessarily* extend to all suppliers and outsourced service-providers: the SCOR standard for supply-chain management extends at the least from supplier's supplier to customer's customer, whilst US legislation mandates control of use of some types of materiel all the way to the end-point of use, regardless of the number of intervening steps. Governance becomes much more complex as soon as it extends beyond organisation boundaries, but engagement in a given market or social context – a given 'vision' – will mandate some themes that must pervade everywhere in that context, and hence will apply to all roles and services in that shared enterprise: the architecture of the enterprise *must* support this requirement, however difficult the governance may be in practice.

Sub-units or variants

As described above, there may be many different types of pervasive services in the enterprise, addressing a very wide range of potential themes; but each service – or service-set – should present essentially the same overall structure.

The three key sub-themes in pervasive-services – creation of awareness of the issues, development of skills and capability, and verification and audit – may sometimes be bundled into the same overall service, but would more often be delivered separately. In some cases separation may be mandated by law or regulation: this would typically be the case for formal auditing and for certification of skills-development. Hence in some models it may be useful to distinguish between the different sub-service types, perhaps by colour-coding; but the same downward-pointing triangle should be used as the base-symbol in each case.

Interfaces

Pervasive-services have three distinct symmetrical connections, as both *provider* and *requester*, with each of their 'customer' services.

The first symmetric-pair connection is with the system-5 'policy' management-service, either at the same level – at the top of the hierarchy-tree – or *at the next level above* – for any pervasive-service instance below that top level. This is a requirements-downward / reporting-upward relationship, similar to that for coordinating-services or the upward link of a management-services set.

The second symmetric-pair link is with the system-3 'direction' management-service at the same level. This is primarily for task-coordination, *not* authorisation or reporting: in particular, it's essential that an audit-service is *not* controlled or managed by the service being audited, as that would defeat the whole object of the audit.

In this sense, the VSM label 'system-3*' is a bit of a misnomer – instead, it really ought to be 'system-5*', to indicate that the primary connection is to the 'policy' management-service. It's probably best to leave the current label alone, though, to avoid breaking any existing use of the VSM elsewhere in the enterprise.

The third symmetric-pair connection is with any or all of the 'child' delivery-services at the current level. This link delivers the service-content of the pervasive-service, and hence will vary with each type of pervasive-service, and the details of the content-type delivered – typically either an audit of some kind, issue-awareness development, or capability-development.

Pervasive services: interfaces with other systems

Note that, as with coordination-services, this differs somewhat from the description in the VSM specification, where system-3* is shown as connecting to the system-3 'direction' service. The key reason for the change here is that, as Patrick Hoverstadt explains in his book on the VSM, system-3* audit *must bypass a management level* in order to do a proper audit of the underlying context of that management-level. The same applies for other pervasive-services: as expressions *of* policy, the primary authority should come *from* system-5 'policy', not system-3 'direction'.

Application

- What purpose does the enterprise serve? What vision does it hold? What values?
- What policies, regulations, law and other social expectations apply to the enterprise from outside?
- What means would be required to keep the enterprise 'on track' to serve each of those chosen or imposed imperatives? What means would be required to ensure that those imperatives are known and understood throughout the enterprise? What means to increase enterprise capabilities to serve those imperatives? What means to report and verify that the enterprise as a whole does indeed serve those imperatives?
- If "the purpose of the system is what it does", what *actual* imperatives does the enterprise serve? Does this vary in different areas of the enterprise – and if so, by how much? Overall, how much, and in what ways, do these 'actual imperatives' differ from the espoused purpose and values? If a gap exists, what services would be needed to close that gap – and also to ensure that it does not re-open?
- What 'anti-services' can you identify in the enterprise? What *architectural* means could you use to minimise their activities and impact?
- In what ways could and should the pervasive-services themselves be monitored? Who watches the watchers?

Resources

📖 Stafford Beer and the Viable System Model: see Stafford Beer, *Brain of the Firm* (Allen Lane: The Penguin Press, 1972)

📖 Viable System Model in organisation design: see Patrick Hoverstadt, *The Fractal Organization: Creating sustainable organizations with the Viable System Model* (Wiley, 2008)

📖 Architecture of pervasive-services: see Tom Graves, *Real Enterprise Architecture: beyond IT to the whole enterprise* (Tetradian, 2008)

PRINCIPLES – PROPERTIES AND PATTERNS

Summary

No service exists in isolation. It exists to serve; it has its own specific nature and properties, each has links and dependencies with other services. A 'systems' perspective helps in making sense of the complexity of all these concerns, by describing patterns of inter-relationships which are known to work in practice. These relationships also clarify options for service re-purpose and re-use, through a concept of 'completeness' as a guide for service design and implementation.

Details

Services as systems

As we've seen, there are many different types of services, each type with its own specific role within the enterprise-as-service. But perhaps the most crucial point is that no service exists in isolation: it is *always* part of a larger system. Hence systems within systems within systems, all the way up to 'the everything'.

> To emphasise the living-enterprise metaphor again, perhaps that ought to be *ecosystem* rather than 'system' – the latter tends to push us back to the old machine-metaphor, which really does start to show its limitations when we get to this level of complexity.
>
> Looking back at that list of characteristics of an IT service-oriented architecture (see p.11), it's clear they make even more sense as views into an ecosystem. Loose-coupling allows a system to adapt and optimise itself to the conditions within its broader ecosystem, and allows the ecosystem itself to adapt to *its* changing context. Each entity within the ecosystem is interchangeable, though only in the sense that system itself also changes with each change of its component members.
>
> And in a living ecosystem, ultimately *everything* is re-composable and re-usable, if only as a compost: in software as in nature, each new generation builds on the foundations provided by its predecessors. Though one nature-metaphor all too common in business that would be useful to *not* use here would be 'red in tooth and claw'. There's a very interesting shift in perspective that occurs when we re-think the

> relationships in an ecosystem's food-chain in terms of services: what services are rendered from prey to predator? – or for that matter, from predator to prey? Kind of eye-opening when we apply that reframing to our own business-ecosystem, too...

To make sense of all this complexity, we need to turn to systems-theory. What it's really about is identifying impacts on the *effectiveness* of the overall system. Yet whilst the full version can be intensely mathematical, to the extent of being impenetrable to anyone other than academics, we can reduce the core down a set of five principles that *are* simple enough to apply in business practice. In our own work we describe these as the R^5 principles:

- *rotation* – review a context from multiple perspectives
- *reciprocation* – balance transactions between services and across the whole ecosystem
- *resonance* – feedback-loops and the like
- *recursion* – patterns of how themes recur at different scales
- *reflexion* – the whole as seen in every part

Rotation is perhaps the most straightforward of these principles: for example, we use it every time we work our way through a checklist – such as this list itself. Those four categories of services – delivery, management, coordination and pervasives, and their respective sub-types, variants and interrelationships – provide probably the most valuable rotation for our purposes here.

Reciprocation means that everything has to balance out somehow. The catch is that this balance may not be direct or immediate, and in many cases may only be achieved over time and over the entire ecosystem, with transfers that can sometimes shift between the physical, conceptual, relational and aspirational dimensions.

> Reciprocation in systems also highlights another serious concern at a much larger scale of business. Our current economic model ultimately relies on an assumption of infinite growth: the catch is that this isn't possible in a closed system – even if that 'system' is as large as an entire planet. In the ecological sense, our so-called 'economy' is not a *viable system*, in any sense of the term.
>
> To be precise, it's in effect a gigantic 'pyramid game' – and pyramid-games can only function for as long as new resources can be pulled in at the base. Ecological analysis suggests that our economy passed that point some fifty years ago: there's certainly no doubt now that it's far overrun its available resources, and that what's left is little more than a shared delusion that's getting more dangerous by the day. Ouch...
>
> So whilst our immediate concern here is the system of an individual enterprise, expect there to be an increasingly rough ride from the

> broader ecosystem within which our enterprise will operate. There's more on the business implications of this, and how to address those implications, in *Power and Response-ability: the human side of systems*, a companion book in this series – see the *Resources* section below.

Resonance would be a favourite theme for almost every systems-theory practitioner. Reciprocation tells us that the system has to balance out somehow; but in reality it frequently does so not in simple win/lose transactions, but in resonant loops that amplify or damp-down the resultant feedback. To complicate the trans-actions even further, there are often delays in those feedback loops, that can range in timescale from microseconds to millennia. Whilst business concerns are likely to be in more visible timescales – from seconds to years – we'll often need to map out those resonant effects so as to be able to see what's actually going on.

Recursion is one of the most valuable items in the system-theory toolkit. Patterns of relationship or interaction repeat or are 'self-similar' at different scales: the 'org-chart' is one obvious example, and the extended 'viable systems' model we're exploring here is another. Whether the system is low-level software, a mid-level process or an entire enterprise, it's always worthwhile watching out for any possible recursion, because it makes our designs much simpler to describe, define and implement.

Reflexion is a somewhat bizarre corollary of recursion, in that in a recursive system, the nature of the whole is also reflected in any and all of its constituent parts. The vision and values of an enter-prise, its policies and purpose, echo all the way down to individual services and sub-services and sub-sub-services – or need to, otherwise what we get is POSIWID. Which is where the pervasive-services come into the picture, and why they are so important to the operation of the enterprise as a whole. But the flipside of this is that wherever we see recursion, we don't have to try to analyse the whole system: we can find out much of its nature just from looking at any part – which again greatly helps to simplify both design, and verification that our designs actually work in the real world.

And that's the aim of viewing services as systems: it gives us a means to improve overall *effectiveness*: efficient, reliable, elegant, appropriate and integrated as an effective enterprise.

Service quality

In service-analysis and design it's all too easy to focus so much on the functional requirements that we forget to pay attention to the so-called 'non-functional' ones. And that can be a *big* mistake...

> 'Non-functional requirement' is an amazing misnomer of a term that's a hangover from the long-forgotten days of 'functional' programming for mainframes. All that it means is that it's a requirement that is not specifically about function – yet it kind of gives the impression that these are the requirements that don't work and therefore don't matter. But that's a serious mistake, because a more accurate term is *'qualitative* requirements' – requirements about quality.
>
> And qualities, and *quality*, most certainly *do* matter in service-design. A service-level agreement is essentially about quality of service. Service-management is mostly about quality of service. The pervasive-services are all about quality in the enterprise. In a competitive environment, an enterprise survives by quality – even price, because price itself is a 'non-functional' quality. Quality *matters*.

One of the difficulties here is that whilst we can indeed describe some qualities in quantitative terms, that isn't the case for all – and yet we need to treat all of the requirements in the same way, or at least to the same level of detail. Often the only way to establish or evaluate a non-numeric quality is through skill and experience – which implies the need for a real person somewhere in the service loop. But in IT-centric contexts, especially where there's a drive to use IT primarily for cost-cutting rather than to improve overall effectiveness of process, there's often a tendency to hide from this fact, or to assume that the IT can handle everything – which it can't. If that happens, there's no way to maintain quality: hence either a poor-quality service, or a service that fails without warning, apparently at random, with no way to see how or why. Quality needs to be designed in from the beginning – and designed in *as* quality.

One way to think about quality – or quali*ties* – is in terms of the pervasive-services. Each of the pervasives represents a 'non-functional requirement' that must be expressed in *everything* in the enterprise: every service must include appropriate support for the security requirements, the environmental requirements, the health and safety requirements, and so on.

> The pervasives *define* what 'quality' *is* for the enterprise: that's *why* they're so important – and why it's so disturbing, and so worrying, that they're so little referenced in most enterprise-architectures and enterprise structures...

We also need to think about quality over the longer term. There's another tendency to think of services only in terms of design-time, as if there's a single static '*the* service', part of the machine: but in reality, each service has its own life-cycle within the living enterprise. Every part of that life-cycle spins off other services, to serve the needs at that specific point: hence, for example, that category of services described earlier as 'change the business' coordinating-services. And every business capability will need some form of maintenance: for software it might be an upgrade, for a manual process it may mean training, for a machine it may just be a quick check-over and a drop of oil here and there; but in every case that too will mean more systems, more services.

A machine doesn't know about quality. It just *is* – and it's maintained from outside itself. A machine the size of an entire enterprise becomes far too complicated to manage: in short, it becomes non-viable. Hence the inevitability of 'wicked problems' for which there seems to be no possible solution, no matter how hard we try to control them.

But a living organism *does* know about quality – and hence can maintain itself, choose its direction, adapt itself to changes in its environment and ecosystem. Hence, in turn, in its analogue of the living enterprise. When the interdependencies become impossibly complex, that emphasis on quality may be the only way we'll stay sane... quality *matters* in the service-oriented enterprise.

Service interdependence

If quality guides our interpretation of interdependencies between services, that interdependence is what enables quality. In a sense, pervasiveness *is* interdependence: a quality is spread through the enterprise by those interdependencies and interconnections. The same is true for infrastructure: whilst the pervasives focus on the 'is' of the enterprise, the infrastructures are coordinating-services that sit *between* delivery-services and the like, and provide support for what the enterprise does, what it knows, how it relates. Each will touch *everywhere*: each often seemingly all but invisible, yet everything in the enterprise will depend on them.

> There's what at first will seem an interesting dilemma here, in that an explicit aim of IT service-orientation, for example, is to minimise cross-dependencies. That's what 'block-box' encapsulation is all about.
>
> But it's not quite the dilemma it seems, because what we're doing here is *exposing* the interfaces to infrastructure and the pervasives – making the 'invisible' visible. That then gives us a new way to handle any

necessary 'hard-wired' cross-dependencies: we change them into messages and suchlike that pass through the now-visible infrastructure – hence the importance of an 'enterprise service-bus' in IT-SOA implementations, or for that matter a light-rail system of some kind to manage the services of a city's commute. Both work because there's 'loose-coupling' through an infrastructure connection that in effect is actually hard-wired.

Service-orientation is not a simple panacea: as in both of those examples, there are several kinds of overhead involved in using the infrastructure, bandwidth can be a real problem, and for some infrastructures creating point-to-point connections for everything can end up impossibly expensive. Relying too much on a single infrastructure can be risky, but duplication can again be too costly in too many ways. Plenty of trade-offs to consider there…

But a true service-orientation allows us to rethink the entire approach by which we might deliver a service. If we need the service of people at work, why do we insist that they must spend perhaps as much as a third of their working lives caught up in the miseries of the daily commute? Why not bring the work to them instead, via alternate infrastructures? That's a core principle behind software-as-a-service, in telecommuting, and in the piecework-assembly processes that are used in so many small manufacturing operations – and in the right contexts, it works very well indeed.

Done well, it also cuts costs all round: yet in the longer term we'll only maintain those savings if we include *all* the pervasive themes of the enterprise – quality-management, security, health-and-safety, all of those other hidden services need to be in place too. So whilst service-orientation is probably essential for the viable enterprise, we need to do it right: a casual, careless, half-hearted approach to services can actually make it *less* viable – which would *not* be a good idea…

Other interdependencies needed for resilience and sustainability can seem more subtle. For example, the VSM indicates that every service must include sub-services for its policy, strategy, direction, coordination, audit and the like, as well as any number of 'child' delivery-services. Unless these are built-in – which many won't within, say, a detail-level IT web-service – then they need to included by reference, as implied links to external services. M such higher-level support-services – particularly for within implementation services at the detail-levels – would necessa provided by people, not IT. For example:

- every service needs an *owner* – the person ultimately responsible for that service
- every service will probably need RACI matrices – lis persons or roles responsible, assists in, to be consul informed about changes

- every service needs *version-identifiers*, to support audit, quality-management, change-management and the like
- every service will probably need CRUD matrices – lists of persons, roles or services that create, retrieve, update or delete content through that service, or instances of the service itself
- every coordinating-service that sits between silos will need management support – in other words, links and transactions with the management-services – at the matching level in the respective silos
- every policy-service will need to link like-with-like to the matching policy-service in 'parent'- and 'child'-services up and down the hierarchy-trees – and likewise for strategy-services
- every pervasive-service must ultimately anchor to a declared quality, value, principle or policy within the enterprise purpose

From a design perspective, these are typical *patterns* that we would expect to see occurring recursively in many different forms at any level and in every aspect of the service-oriented enterprise.

'afford Beer also asserted that every service might also need
't he termed 'algedonic' links with any – or even every – other
'e. These connections are point-to-point, bypassing the usual
'unication-channels via the management hierarchy-trees.

'eneral, algedonic links should be reserved for emergencies only, in
'ecause the requirement for point-to-point connections breaches
'se-coupling principle and could add enormous complexity to a
'. though that concern is eased if a suitable infrastructure
'ists to carry them, such as matching email, phone and URL-
's to a help-desk service. 'Algedonic' literally means 'pain-
'nce the 'audit' component of the pervasive-services also
'of algedonic channel, identifying the respective type of
're' within the system.

'iddle-managers often *hate* algedonic links: they bypass
'uthority, and as a result may often seem *personally*
'it or not, such connections are *essential* to the
'-oriented enterprise: the 'normal channels' are
'ope with emergencies, and without the
'prise will crash and burn.

'ican some years back described a variety of
'electricity power-distribution and aircraft-
'of the examples – all of which used
'ement-structure. Each had a strict
'ilities: everyone knew their place, in

necessary 'hard-wired' cross-dependencies: we change them into messages and suchlike that pass through the now-visible infrastructure – hence the importance of an 'enterprise service-bus' in IT-SOA implementations, or for that matter a light-rail system of some kind to manage the services of a city's commute. Both work because there's 'loose-coupling' through an infrastructure connection that in effect is actually hard-wired.

Service-orientation is not a simple panacea: as in both of those examples, there are several kinds of overhead involved in using the infrastructure, bandwidth can be a real problem, and for some infrastructures creating point-to-point connections for everything can end up impossibly expensive. Relying too much on a single infrastructure can be risky, but duplication can again be too costly in too many ways. Plenty of trade-offs to consider there...

But a true service-orientation allows us to rethink the entire approach by which we might deliver a service. If we need the service of people at work, why do we insist that they must spend perhaps as much as a third of their working lives caught up in the miseries of the daily commute? Why not bring the work to them instead, via alternate infrastructures? That's a core principle behind software-as-a-service, in telecommuting, and in the piecework-assembly processes that are used in so many small manufacturing operations – and in the right contexts, it works very well indeed.

Done well, it also cuts costs all round: yet in the longer term we'll only maintain those savings if we include *all* the pervasive themes of the enterprise – quality-management, security, health-and-safety, all of those other hidden services need to be in place too. So whilst service-orientation is probably essential for the viable enterprise, we need to do it right: a casual, careless, half-hearted approach to services can actually make it *less* viable – which would *not* be a good idea...

Other interdependencies needed for resilience and sustainability can seem more subtle. For example, the VSM indicates that every service must include sub-services for its policy, strategy, direction, coordination, audit and the like, as well as any number of 'child' delivery-services. Unless these are built-in – which many won't be within, say, a detail-level IT web-service – then they need to be included by reference, as implied links to external services. Many such higher-level support-services – particularly for within the implementation services at the detail-levels – would necessarily be provided by people, not IT. For example:

- every service needs an *owner* – the person ultimately responsible for that service
- every service will probably need RACI matrices – lists of persons or roles responsible, assists in, to be consulted or informed about changes

- every service needs *version-identifiers*, to support audit, quality-management, change-management and the like
- every service will probably need CRUD matrices – lists of persons, roles or services that create, retrieve, update or delete content through that service, or instances of the service itself
- every coordinating-service that sits between silos will need management support – in other words, links and transactions with the management-services – at the matching level in the respective silos
- every policy-service will need to link like-with-like to the matching policy-service in 'parent'- and 'child'-services up and down the hierarchy-trees – and likewise for strategy-services
- every pervasive-service must ultimately anchor to a declared quality, value, principle or policy within the enterprise purpose

From a design perspective, these are typical *patterns* that we would expect to see occurring recursively in many different forms at any level and in every aspect of the service-oriented enterprise.

Stafford Beer also asserted that every service might also need what he termed 'algedonic' links with any – or even every – other service. These connections are point-to-point, bypassing the usual communication-channels via the management hierarchy-trees.

In general, algedonic links should be reserved for emergencies only, in part because the requirement for point-to-point connections breaches the loose-coupling principle and could add enormous complexity to a system – though that concern is eased if a suitable infrastructure already exists to carry them, such as matching email, phone and URL-address links to a help-desk service. 'Algedonic' literally means 'pain-pleasure', hence the 'audit' component of the pervasive-services also acts as a kind of algedonic channel, identifying the respective type of 'pain' or 'pleasure' within the system.

Unsurprisingly, middle-managers often *hate* algedonic links: they bypass the formal trail of authority, and as a result may often seem *personally* threatening. But like it or not, such connections are *essential* to the viability of the service-oriented enterprise: the 'normal channels' are invariably too slow to cope with emergencies, and without the algedonic links, the enterprise will crash and burn.

An article in *Scientific American* some years back described a variety of high-stress environments – electricity power-distribution and aircraft-carrier flight-deck were two of the examples – all of which used exactly the same kind of management-structure. Each had a strict hierarchy of ranks and responsibilities: everyone knew their place, in

every sense of that term – because that gave the greatest efficiency under 'normal' high-stress conditions. But at the same time, *everyone* was also able to connect with anyone else for emergency purposes: even the lowest-ranking erks on the aircraft-carrier had the authority *and duty* to call the admiral direct if they thought that the ship was at risk for any reason. Hence neither a true rigid hierarchy, nor a true 'flat' management-structure, but a kind of 'hierarchy/flat' somewhere in between, incorporating the best features of both, and creating a *responsibility-driven* enterprise: that's what the algedonic links allow.

And following the same recursion, every link between services – every interdependency – is implicitly a link which also connects the physical, the conceptual, the relational and the aspirational dimensions of the context: in other words, the things, knowledge, people and purpose that apply in that context. Every link is about information; every link is about trust, about quality; and every link must exist in some form, physical, virtual or otherwise.

This may at first sound somewhat abstract, but it has real practical implications for the service-oriented enterprise: for example, if every VSM link implies a need for some kind of information-transfer, the model is therefore also inherently a known-proven pattern for IT-system design. The pervasive links in turn emphasise the importance of other key IT themes such as 'database of record', 'single sign-on' and 'single source of truth' – often difficult to implement in practice, but all of them essential to overall quality in the service-oriented enterprise.

Service completeness

Another type of pattern we need to watch for is architectural *completeness*. To put it in its simplest form, services are usable to the extent that they're architecturally complete, yet also *re*-usable to the extent that they're architecturally *in*complete. Given the natural recursion of services, we know that enterprise viability will depend on the presence of all the support-services, and on the effectiveness of the interfaces between them. But to *re-use* services – that key concept of loose-coupling – we also need to be able to split them apart, to make services temporarily 'incomplete'.

> Viability depends on completeness;
> Re-use depends on incompleteness

'Incomplete' services become design-patterns, or implementation-patterns. Those principles of loose-coupling and encapsulation are themselves design-patterns for intentional 'incompletion', to be resolved at run-time: the connections and service-contracts create the 'completion' needed to make service-delivery happen.

At this point we need to link to another related architectural issue around completeness. A service is a combination of capability and function, yet this is only part of a more generic pattern for viable completeness at the implementation level:

"with «*asset*» do «*function*» at «*location*»
using «*capability*» on «*event*» because «*reason*»"

In principle, we should be able to describe the implementation-completeness of *everything* in terms of that one sentence-structure. It's derived from an expansion of the well-known Zachman framework, which extends the original with an extra row at the top for enterprise core-constants or 'universals', and an extra dimension to clarify scope and actual implementation.

Framework rows, columns and segments

> The framework is described in more detail in a companion volume in this series, *Bridging the Silos: enterprise architecture for IT-architects* – see the *Resources* section below.

For the vertical dimension of the framework, we partition scope in terms of timescale – a set of seven distinct layers or perspectives, from unchanging constants, to items which change moment by moment. Each row adds another concern or attribute:

- *Row 0:* '**Universals**' – in principle, should never change: core constants to which everything should align – identifies the overall region of interest and the key points of connection shared with enterprise partners and other stakeholders; provides compatibility with ISO-9000 etc

- *Row 1*: **'Scope'** (*Zachman*: 'Planner') – adds possibility of change, if usually slowly: core entities in each category, in list form, *without* relationships – the key 'items of interest' for the enterprise
- *Row 2*: **'Business'** (*Zachman*: 'Owner') – adds relationships and dependencies between entities: core entities described in summary-form for business-metrics, including relationships between entities both of the same type ('primitives') and of different types ('composites')
- *Row 3*: **'System'** (*Zachman*: 'Designer') – adds attributes to abstract 'logical' entities: entities expanded out into implementation-*independent* designs – includes descriptive attributes
- *Row 4*: **'Develop'** (*Zachman*: 'Builder') – adds details for real-world 'physical' design: entities and attributes expanded out into implementation-*dependent* designs, including additional patterns such as cross-reference tables for 'many-to-many' data-relationships
- *Row 5*: **'Implement'** (*Zachman*: 'Sub-contractor' or 'Out of Scope') – adds details of intended future deployment: implementation of designs into actual software, actual business-processes, work-instructions, hardware, networks etc
- *Row 6*: **'Operations'** (*Zachman*: implied but not described) – adds details of actual usage: specific instances of entities, processes etc, as created, modified, and acted on in real-time operations

The rows also represent different categories of responsibilities or stakeholders, such as senior management responsible for row-0 universals, or strategists at row-1 and -2, architects and solution-designers at row-3 and -4, and line managers and front-line staff at row-5 and -6. In effect, this is the same layering that we see in the management-hierarchy, and in the nesting of abstract services.

Below the core 'Universals', the framework splits horizontally into columns for six distinct categories of primitives, approximating to Zachman's what, how, where, who, when and why:

- *What*: **assets** of any kind – physical objects, data, links to people, morale, finances, etc
- *How*: **functions** – activities or services to create change, described independently from the agent (machine, software, person etc) that carries out that activity

- *Where*: **locations** – in physical space (geography etc), virtual space (IP nodes, http addresses etc), relational space (social networks etc), time and suchlike
- *Who*: **capabilities** clustered as **roles** or 'actors' – may be human, machine, software application, etc, and individual or collective
- *When*: **events** and relationships between those events – may be in time, or physical, virtual, human, business-rule trigger or other event
- *Why*: **decisions**, reasons, constraints and tests which trigger or validate the condition for the 'reason', as in strategy, policy, business-requirements, business-rules, regulations etc.

In the lower layers, we also need to split the columns themselves by context into distinct segments or sub-categories. Whilst these could be cut multiple ways, a typical set of segments would be:

- **physical**: tangible objects (What), mechanical processes (How), physical or temporal locations (Where), physical events (When); also align to *rule-based* skills (Who) and decisions (Why)
- **virtual**: intangible objects such as data (What), software processes (How), logical locations (Where), data-events (When); also align to *analytic* skills (Who) and decisions (Why)
- **relational**: links to people (What), manual processes (How), social/relational locations (Where), human events (When); also align to *heuristic* skills (Who) and decisions (Why)
- **aspirational**: principles and values (What), value-webs and dependencies (Where), business-rules (When); also align with *principle-based* skills (Who) and decisions (Why)
- **abstract**: additional uncategorised segments such as financial (What, How), energy (What) etc

Relationships or 'composites' may exist in columns between items in the same segment, or in different segments. We link composites across other columns to create 'incomplete' design-patterns, or complete the composite across all columns for final implementation. This balance between incompletion and completion enables architectural redesign, anchoring trails of relationship between items or layers, to resolve business-concerns such as strategic analysis, failure-impact analysis and complex 'pain-points'.

Which is where we come back to service-oriented architecture and the service-oriented enterprise, because the layering of services – particularly the management-services – maps well onto the layering of the framework; and services themselves are ready-made design-composites that already straddle at least two of the framework columns – function and capability – and often map easily onto others such as 'event' and 'asset'. The two columns that don't map so easily are 'location' – which is usually an issue around implementation rather than at design-time – and 'decision'. Yet the latter is where the pervasive-services come back into the picture, because their role centres around the 'why' of the enterprise.

So in turn we need to review each of the enterprise pervasive-services in terms of each of the segments of the framework; or each of the tetradian dimensions – physical, conceptual, relational, aspirational – since it comes to much the same in practice. For example, consider the pervasive-services which focus on security. The basic assumption, especially in an IT context, would be that it's essentially about 'need to know' – the conceptual dimension. In the machine-metaphor for the enterprise we might also acknowledge a 'need to use' – the physical dimension. Yet that's still only the start: in the living-organism metaphor we learn to recognise that security becomes 'viable' only when we include *all* the tetradian dimensions:

- *physical*: need to *use*, need to have access
- *conceptual*: need to *know*, need to learn
- *relational*: need to *connect*, to relate, interact or talk with other
- *aspirational*: need to *belong*, to share common vision and values

In each dimension, there are consequences of allowing security to be too open. The catch is that those consequences may be felt only in what would otherwise appear to be unconnected aspects of the security context. In the case of email, for example, lax attitudes to relational-security concerns such as rampant forwarding and 'for-information' copies has a huge cost not just in people's time dealing with email-glut – "too much information!" – but also in disk-storage, bandwidth and similar physical-dimension themes. It's not a 'need to know' issue, but it does need to be understood in the same kind of terms: it's an *overall security* issue, that needs to be resolved through appropriate pervasive-services – in this case, education to shift the culture around the over-use of email. And often those cultural issues may echo back and forth into other dimensions: in that example, the real driver might be a climate of fear, with everyone trying to spread responsibility for difficult decisions as far around the enterprise as possible. Pervasive themes are literally pervasive: they impact everywhere in the enterprise, and often in unexpected ways.

Yet there are also consequences to setting security too tight in any dimension – and again, the real impacts may become apparent only in other dimensions. For example, if we shut people off from information that they believe they need for their work, they not only make poorer decisions, but they also lose their sense of belonging to the enterprise – which is likely to have serious impacts on commitment and morale and other aspirational-dimension themes. If we become too obsessed about physical security, such as an over-dominant health-and-safety focus, we end up creating a context in which people not only can't do their work – physical-dimension – but also can't learn the requisite skills – conceptual-dimension and aspirational-dimension – and may well become *more* at risk because they don't understand the dangers, inventing unsafe workarounds just to get things done.

So service-completeness applies not just to patterns for design and re-use, but to the broader architectural assessment as well. The recursive approach we've used above also inherently acts as a gap-analysis to identify and highlight potential holes in the viability of service-designs and service-structures, and in the enterprise as a whole. And as we move now from principles to practice, we'll start to see how all of these concerns would apply in the real world of the service-oriented enterprise.

Application

- In what ways would you apply the R^5 principles – rotation, reciprocation, resonance, recursion and reflexion – in architecture-assessment for your own enterprise? Given that some of these concepts may seem alien to 'business as usual' thinking, how would you express to others what these tools will show you about the enterprise and its services?

- In what ways does the perspective shift when you replace the term 'non-functional requirements' with 'qualitative requirements'? In what ways do the priorities for solution-designs shift as you do so? For example, do qualitative concerns start to seem more important than before? If so, what could you do to respond to those changed priorities?

- What are the interdependencies between systems in your own enterprise? How would you map the interactions across those links, at each level and within and between each silo in the enterprise? By what means could you use the 'service' paradigm to identify and simplify those interfaces?
- What patterns do you identify in your existing system designs and system implementations? In what ways do such patterns enable re-purpose and re-use? How do you balance 'completion' and 'incompletion' – especially in service-design and service-implementation?
- Your existing security-models and security-management for the enterprise will cover 'need to know', and probably 'need to use'; but to what extent do they also address 'need to relate' and 'need to belong'? What happens to your perception of security overall when you add those extra dimensions to the security picture? What – if anything – can you see that would need to change when you *do* include those dimensions?

Resources

📖 R[5] systems-theory principles: see chapter 'Architecture as a way of thinking' (and overall book-structure) in Tom Graves, *Real Enterprise Architecture: beyond IT to the whole enterprise* (Tetradian, 2008)

📖 Business-oriented introduction to systems-thinking: see Peter Senge, *The Fifth Discipline: The Art & Practice of the Learning Organization* (Doubleday, 1990)

📖 Applications of systems-thinking techniques to organisational change: see Peter Senge, *The Dance of Change: The Challenges of Sustaining Momentum in Learning Organizations* (Nicholas Brealey Publishing, 1999)

🏯 Online resources on 'Fifth Discipline': see www.fieldbook.com

📖 Business implications of economy-as-system: see Tom Graves, *Power and Response-ability: the human side of systems* (Tetradian, 2008)

🏯 Zachman framework: see www.zifa.com

📖 Framework for whole-of-enterprise and service architecture: see chapters 'Framework – Layers' and 'Framework – Primitives' in Tom Graves, *Bridging the Silos: enterprise architecture for IT-architects* (Tetradian, 2008)

PRACTICE – AN OVERVIEW

The service-oriented enterprise is composed of a myriad of other services at many different scales. We can describe each of these as belonging to one of four categories: delivery, management, co-ordination and pervasive quality:

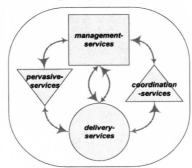

Four categories of services

But in itself this doesn't tell us much about how the services inter-relate with each other in practice; and it also doesn't tell us much about how to describe that real-world practice. For those, our best tactic would be to merge that four-fold service-structure with another five-phase approach to modelling and mapping the archi-tecture of the enterprise:

Four categories, five phases

> This methodology is described in more depth in another companion
> volume in this series, *Real Enterprise Architecture: beyond IT to the whole
> enterprise* – see the *Resources* section below.

So this Practice section is split into five chapters, each describing aspects of service-architecture and the service-oriented enterprise in terms of the respective phase:

- *purpose*: an emphasis on pervasive-services: "what purpose does the enterprise serve? whom does it serve?" – see *Practice – Service purpose*, p.94

- *people*: an emphasis on management-services: "how do services relate with each other?" – see *Practice – Services and functions*, p.102

- *preparation*: an emphasis on coordination-services: "what do services know and need to know?" – see *Practice – The knowledge of services*, p.113

- *process*: an emphasis on delivery-services: "what does each service do? how does it do it? how do we coordinate services to get real work done?" – see *Practice – Services in action*, p.122

- *performance*: an emphasis again on pervasive-services: "what have we done? how can we improve what we do?" – see *Practice – Optimising services*, p.133

Although this cannot cover every possible aspect of service architecture, of course, it should provide enough to begin to put the principles into real practice within the architecture of your own present enterprise.

Resources

📖 Recursive five-phase enterprise-architecture: see chapter 'An overview' and overall book-structure in Tom Graves, *Real Enterprise Architecture: beyond IT to the whole enterprise* (Tetradian, 2008)

PRACTICE – SERVICE PURPOSE

Summary

The first question for any service-architecture is "whom do we serve?" The answers identify the overall purpose for the services provided by the enterprise-as-service, and the anchors for the architectures that support that need.

Details

Business as a service

To the service-oriented enterprise, the enterprise itself is a service. Yet if it's a service, *whom* does it serve? What *is* the service? What is the *purpose* of the enterprise? Such questions barely matter in the machine-metaphor: after all, it's just a machine... But in the organism-metaphor, those questions go right to the core of the enterprise: the answers to those questions are the *reasons* for its existence.

Application themes: enterprise as service

- Whom does your enterprise serve?
- What purpose does it serve?
- In what ways does it serve?

> In commercial organisations especially, it's easy to fall prey to cynicism here: "we exist to make the shareholders rich...". That kind of feeling is understandably endemic wherever the Taylorist machine-metaphor dominates: but in the organism-metaphor it's essential to break free from the cynicism, and instead really explore what it is that brings the enterprise alive.
>
> What role does it play in 'the wider scheme of things'? If it's a commercial enterprise, ignore the shareholders for a moment – to be blunt, their real business function is merely that of service-providers, for one specific type of resource that the enterprise will need – and concentrate instead on the value-webs in which the enterprise participates. Who are the 'customers' here, and in which parts of the value-web? A focus there will give you a clearer set of answers as to whom and for what the enterprise truly exists to serve.

In practice it may take several iterations through those questions before arriving at answers that seem genuinely meaningful across the enterprise. A classic cue is that an authentic answer will have a kind of emotive resonance, a sense of 'rightness' about it – though again, don't expect to arrive at it on the very first try.

If you're using a purpose-built architecture toolset, place the answers as entities in the row-0 'Universals' section of the architecture framework (see p.86). In any case, document the results for later review.

Application themes: stakeholders

- Extending 'whom does the enterprise serve', who are the stakeholders in the enterprise?
- What are the aims, needs, purpose for each of these stakeholders?
- What are the common factors between each of these stakeholders? What is the shared 'guiding star' that links all of the stakeholders together?

The distinction here is between 'value-chain' and 'value-web'. The conventional notion about business-value is that there's a single chain of 'added value' between customer and profit. That is, as usual, a very machine-like way of looking at the issues: in reality, those issues are a great more complex, because the customers – like the shareholders, for that matter – are just one group amongst many who have an active 'stake' in the wellbeing of the enterprise. To take a classic supply-chain view, the stakeholders would include everyone from supplier's supplier to customer's customer; and to those we would need to add all the service-providers, and everyone employed by the enterprise, either directly or indirectly; all the families of those people; everyone living in the vicinity of the enterprise workplaces; local governments and legislative or regulatory bodies; the list goes on and on. To make sense of that vast inventory of conflicting interests, look for a common 'guiding star' that links them all: that in turn will give you a clearer pointer to the questions about whom and how the enterprise serves.

Application themes: stakeholder imbalance

- Are any specific stakeholders 'privileged' above all others?
- If so, who? What imbalances does this cause in the ways the enterprise can serve?
- What could you do in your architecture to redress any such imbalances?

> In many contexts even to ask such questions, let alone act on them, may well seem fraught and politically-loaded, to say the least...

> But whilst you're unlikely to have much authority to make changes
> here, as an architect you *do* have the authority — and responsibility — to
> identify the impacts of such imbalances, and at least suggest what could
> be done, in terms of enterprise *structure*, to ameliorate those impacts.
> If any stakeholder has a role that's little better than a parasite, in terms
> of the organism-metaphor, then as enterprise-architect it's your *duty*
> to say so, because that one parasite could well kill the whole
> enterprise, to everyone's loss — including that of the parasite.
>
> So whilst these questions may seem simple at first, they do go right to
> the core of the enterprise. Not trivial at all...

As before, document the answers in the 'row-0 universals' section of the framework, and perhaps also use them to review the results from the previous questions.

Application themes: vision and values

- What values do each of the stakeholders bring to that shared common purpose?
- What commonalities and conflicts exist between all these different values?
- What values does the enterprise need so as to fulfil its part in that shared purpose?
- What values does the enterprise currently express – perhaps as indicated by POSIWID?
- What impacts do any value-mismatches have on the effectiveness of the enterprise in moving towards its espoused aims?
- What would need to be done to ameliorate those impacts? What would need to be done to bring the current actual values in line with those needed?

> Once again, as an enterprise architect, you may not have the authority
> to do anything directly about any values-issues. But you *do* have the
> authority and ability to identify their impacts, and perhaps describe to
> others what could be done in structural terms to address them.

Use values-mapping and requirements-modelling techniques to identify enterprise values and their commonalities and conflicts. Document the results in the 'universals' part of the framework.

Techniques such as VPEC-T, SCORE and even classic SWOT analysis will be helpful in identifying the impacts of any values-conflicts.

- What policies will need to apply throughout the enterprise in order to support the vision and espoused values?
- What laws, regulations, standards, policies and other external constraints will apply to the enterprise from the social and business milieu within which it exists and operates?

Again, requirements-modelling and techniques such as VPEC-T and SCORE will be useful to map these policies and constraints, and the cross-dependencies and conflicts between them.

Document the results as per the applicable architecture principles and practices: for example, if you're using a Zachman-style framework, these would typically go into row-1, row-2 or even row-3 of the 'why' or 'reasons' column. Cross-link each of these references back to the appropriate items in the row-0 vision and values.

The structure of purpose

The vision, values, principles and constraints form the ultimate anchors for the pervasive-services, and in turn also for the trails of performance metrics to be tracked via the management-services.

One common tool for modelling the relationships between these factors is the Business Motivation Model (BMM), developed by the Business Rules Group and now maintained as a formal standard by the Object Management Group (OMG). In our experience, though, it has a few serious flaws – particularly in its handling of the 'vision' layer. For strategy with broader scope, we would usually supplement the BMM with an additional layering of Vision, Role, Mission and Goal:

- *Vision*: a short statement describing a desired 'world' or world-condition that engages and encompasses the common interests of all its stakeholders; always greater in scope than the organisation itself
- *Role*: a description of what the organisation will do, and will not do, in support of the aims of the Vision's 'world'
- *Mission*: a description of a capability to support the Role, which the organisation will create, maintain and, eventually, dismantle as appropriate
- *Goal*: a description of a 'project' or equivalent, in support of a Mission, with specific deliverables, specific requirements for resources and a specific target completion-date

Ultimately, for every activity in the organisation, we should be able to identify an audit-trail of its parent Goal, Mission and Role, all the way back up to the enterprise Vision.

Layering of ends and means: vision, role, mission, goal

If we view the whole organisation as a single delivery-service, what it serves is the Vision. What it does as a service is deliver its Role, in conjunction with the Role-services delivered by all the other stakeholders. The top-level management is contained within that single top-level delivery-service; the Vision is the anchor for the enterprise pervasive-services; and the Role acts as an identifier for the inter-enterprise coordination-services.

Each value-chain in the enterprise – there may be several of them – is served by an ongoing Mission, which itself is a delivery-service on the next layer down in the service-hierarchy. Each of these may be served by many other internal Missions, capabilities, within the myriad of sub-enterprises and sub-sub-enterprises within the broader enterprise. In turn, each Goal is an individual, measurable, finite step within the delivery-processes of a Mission.

Application themes: vision, role, mission, goal

- What is the Vision for your enterprise? – the broader 'world' which all its stakeholders share, and whose aims they hold in common?
- What Role – or Roles – does the organisation play in that 'world'? What Roles does it *not* play, and hence leaves open for exchange with other stakeholders in that 'world'?
- What Missions are required to support the organisation's Role(s)? What forms do those Missions take within the enterprise? In what ways do those Missions change over time?

- What Goals are required to support those Missions? How do you monitor that each Goal has been achieved? How do you ensure that each Goal is 'on purpose', all the way back to the original Vision?

In principle, the enterprise has only one Vision; and in principle, it should never change, because if it does, it ceases to be same enterprise. The Role – or Roles – may change slowly over time; the Missions may change more often, morphing somewhat with each change in technology or business-context or whatever; and Goals come and go according to their own timescales. But underlying each of these is the same notion of *service*:

Application themes: mission and service

- Whom does each Mission serve? How do you identify and verify these connections?
- What needs does each Mission serve? How do you identify and verify these needs?
- What is the content of each Mission transaction? How do you identify and verify what this content should be?
- How do you identify and verify that the need has been served in each service-transaction?

Which leads us to a matter of metrics. As we've seen, these are collected initially at the root transaction-layer, and are collated and aggregated as they move upward through the management-services tree. We measure each Goal on completion; we measure each Mission on a continual basis, at regular intervals and verified through occasional audit.

Those metrics then travel back *down* the hierarchy-tree via the pervasive-services, to complete the feedback loops for service-monitoring and service-improvement. But how do we know that we have the right metrics in the first place? To do that, we still need the sense of the enterprise as a single unified service:

Application themes: mission, goal and metrics

- What metrics do you collect for each Goal? For what purpose? In what ways do these help to improve the performance of subsequent Goals?
- What metrics do you collect for each Mission? At what intervals? What kinds of audit-processes do you need, to verify those metrics?

- How are those metrics transformed as they pass up the management-services tree? Into what abstractions and aggregates? What purpose does each transform serve?
- How are those metrics re-used in subsequent audit, passing back down the pervasive-services trees? How do they help to complete the respective feedback-loops for performance-monitoring?
- How are those metrics re-used for service-improvement? How does that re-use align with the business-purpose of each service, and the overall purpose of the enterprise as service?

If the management-services represent 'the brain of the firm', the pervasive-services are its heart or soul – its means for staying 'on purpose' in relation to the Vision. The enterprise values form the ultimate anchors for the trees of pervasive-services:

Application themes: staying on purpose

- How do the enterprise values support the Vision? What values are needed in order to support that Vision? And by what means would you identify and address any implicit values that would pull the enterprise away from the Vision?
- What pervasive-services are needed to support each required enterprise value? How do the respective pervasive-service trees devolve from each enterprise value?
- By what means do the pervasive-services extend throughout the entire enterprise?
- What combinations of awareness-development, capability-development and audit are required at each layer and in each context? How do these combinations, and the content of each combination, change in differing contexts?
- By what means would you verify that each instance of a pervasive-service supports its respective parent enterprise-value, all the way up the value-tree to the enterprise Vision?
- Viewing the entire enterprise as a single service, what else would you need to do or define, to ensure that that service remains 'on purpose' in relation to the Vision?

These questions may seem abstract at first, but they form the underlying foundation of 'enterprise *as* service' for the service-oriented enterprise.

100

Resources

📖 Strategic role of enterprise-architecture: see Jeanne W. Ross, Peter Weill and David Robertson, *Enterprise Architecture As Strategy: Creating a Foundation for Business Execution* (Harvard Business Press, 2008)

📖 Enterprise values: see Michael Henderson and Dougal Thompson, *Values At Work: the invisible threads between people, performance and profit* (HarperBusiness New Zealand, 2003)

📖 Mapping of requirements and constraints: see Suzanne Robertson and James Robertson, *Mastering the Requirements Process* (Addison-Wesley, 1999)

📖 Values-mapping with VPEC-T: see Nigel Green and Carl Bate, *Lost In Translation: a handbook for information systems in the 21st century* (Evolved Media, 2007)

📖 SCORE strategy-analysis: see chapter 'SCORE for strategy' in Tom Graves, *SEMPER and SCORE: enhancing enterprise effectiveness* (Tetradian, 2008)

📖 Layering of vision, role, mission, goal: see chapter 'Architecture on purpose' in Tom Graves, *Real Enterprise Architecture: beyond IT to the whole enterprise* (Tetradian, 2008)

🕸 Business Motivation Model: see businessrulesgroup.org/bmm.shtml

PRACTICE – SERVICES AND FUNCTIONS

Summary

With purpose identified, the next architecture requirement is the definition of the services needed to implement it. In doing so, we need to map how these services would interrelate with each other – particularly the people-aspects of the enterprise. One proven tactic is to create a Functional Business Model as a base-map for subsequent explorations.

Details

Function as service, service as function

In mathematical terms, a *function* is something that can create a change in accordance with intent. The same is true in business too: and especially at the upper levels of the enterprise, 'function' is almost synonymous with 'service'. Business-functions *are* services.

So how do we describe how these functions or services interrelate with each other? The layering of delivery-services – the business functions – is also a layering of the management-services and their resultant silos; and the various ways in which those delivery-services link together across the silos also describes the layering and interactions of the 'run the business' coordination-services. In that sense, functions describe the enterprise itself.

So a Functional Business Model is one of the most valuable tools for architecture of the service-oriented enterprise. Once we have the vision and values clearly described, as the anchors for everything else, the next item we'll need is that function-model.

The Functional Business Model

A Functional Business Model is a layered list of business functions – a visual summary of what the enterprise does in functional or service terms. So the aim here is to create a model that remains much the same as long as the enterprise does that kind of work.

For that reason, the content of the model needs to be independent of the current structure of the enterprise. So in a sense we run the usual enterprise-architecture process backwards here: we start with the 'to-be' model, the description of the idealised enterprise, and then work backwards from there to link it to what actually exists in the present day. That in turn will give us the gap-analysis that we'll need for future change towards that 'to-be' ideal.

The aim is that the model should summarise the whole enterprise on a single page. Although it would fit best on a larger sheet (A3 or 11x17), it should still be readable on a standard single sheet (A4 or 8½x11). In this form, and at this size, it supports understanding across the enterprise, at a 'big picture' level. In effect, it provides a high-level visual anchor for the enterprise's business-architecture.

> Remember that an 'enterprise' here can be at any scale: any subset or superset of an organisation. But when the model works well, it provides an instant overview of the whole enterprise, at whatever scale that may be.
>
> In one case, we saw a copy of the model pinned up on the wall in almost every manager's office. It guides conversations about end-to-end processes, or any process that crosses boundaries between organisational silos – a process being in effect a choreographed path that links business services together to *do* something that contributes towards the organisation's goals.

With a completed function-model, you can allocate functions to *business systems* – clusters of activities that do similar things and share similar information in different areas of the enterprise. This simplifies mapping of applications and systems across the whole of the enterprise. You can also map projects and applications to functions, allowing you to see gaps and overlaps in the system coverage, and identify potential for new projects. And by cross-mapping to activity-based costing, you can map costs to functions, highlighting the targeting of project spend. That's a lot of value from one relatively simple model.

The model is laid out in whatever format best describes the business. It could be laid out as a left-to-right flow from 'Customer' to 'Delivery', with supporting activities above and below, as in the first of the examples shown later in this chapter, on p.109; it could be laid out as an open box; or any other layout that feels right and makes sense as a business description. But whatever layout is used, it's typically organised as a visual nested hierarchy, usually with three or four tiers of functions:

- **Tier 1**: major categories of business functions.- key aspects of what the enterprise as a whole actually *does*.
- **Tier 2**: clusters of related activities – the major support-missions for the tier-1 functions
- **Tier 3**: 'activities' or clusters of related tasks – typically the emphasis of a team's or a person's work.
- **Tier 4**: the individual tasks within business processes – the actual delivery-processes

The tier-4 functions are usually not shown on the diagram, for lack of space, but instead would be listed within a supporting text document. Although there is real value to be gained from gathering the full information at every tier, the cost of doing so rises with the level of detail. The first three tiers are probably essential for any enterprise-modelling exercise, but it's likely that tier-4 information may be worth gathering in depth only when an appropriate project touches the respective area of the enterprise.

Creating a Function Model

A few key points need to be kept in mind throughout the process of creating a function-model:

- the model needs to be independent of the current organisational structure or business units – for example, an org-chart is effect an *overlay* on the Function Model
- the model needs to be independent of any existing applications – because they are likely to change in future
- each function or activity in effect delivers a service

To identify candidate functions and activities, trawl through existing documents such as org-charts, strategies, plans and annual reports, and also intranet sites and the like. Look for:

- org-chart entries: each role implies one or more business functions – though they may overlap, or be repeated in multiple locations, or aggregate several distinct functions
- references to projects: each is likely to imply a new or upgraded capability, which again implies a function
- references to phone-lines or other contact-points: these imply business-functions behind the points of contact

It's also a good idea to build a network of business acquaintances to help you fill in any gaps. One of my standard tactics is to sit in whatever café is used by staff to get their morning coffee, with a cluster of interesting-looking diagrams casually laid out on the table as

Another source of pointers to functions is the business data. If an enterprise data-model is available, trawl through that, looking for the implied functions that would create, read, aggregate, update or delete the information-items.

Every business function *does* something, so each function-label on the model should begin with or include a verb. For the tier-1 and tier-2 functions it would be acceptable to use abstract verbs such as 'Provide' or 'Manage', but wherever practicable, and for tier-3 or tier-4 especially, it's advisable to use more specific, descriptive verbs such as 'Receive', 'Assess', 'Monitor' and so on.

Application themes: tier-1 functions

- What are the major categories of business functions?
- How do these functions relate with each other, in terms of service-categories and service-layering?

Aim to define some six to twelve tier-1 functions. These will usually be obvious in the structure of the enterprise: for example, every organisation will have a set of 'business support' functions such as HR and finance, a set of contact-points for customers and other stakeholders, a layer for strategy and management, and a set of core business-processes.

Functions: tier-1 example

Application themes: tier-2 functions

For each tier-1 category:

- What are the main clusters of related activities that occur within this category?
- How do these functions relate with each other, in terms of service-categories and service-layering?

Expect to identify around 40 to 50 of these in total. They can sometimes be found from job-titles: a truck driver, for example, or a warehouse manager, who each do a range of related business activities and tasks. The org-chart will also give some pointers on this, though again take care not to tie the list too tightly to anything that's likely to change.

Functions: tier-2 example

Functions at tier-2 can be harder to identify than those at tier-3 and below: the latter can be detected readily via a trawl through documents and the like. To derive tier-2 functions, look for natural clusterings of tier-3 functions: often these will be implied by higher-level entries in the org-chart, or by groupings of functions that reappear together in different geographical locations.

Application themes: tier-3 functions

For each tier-2 cluster of related activities:

- What are the main 'activities' or clusters of related tasks?
- How do these functions relate with each other, in terms of service-categories and service-layering?

Tier-3 'activities' typically represent the main emphasis of a single person's work. Aim to identify 200 to 300 of these – perhaps less in a smaller organisation, but not more, in case the model becomes too complicated to make sense.

106

Functions: tier-3 example

A warning: human nature being what it is, *every* manager will want you to list every one of their business functions on the diagram... You'll need to apply some fairly strong negotiating skills to get the balance right across the whole organisation, because there'll never be enough space to list *everything!* As a guide to negotiation, set yourself a strict limit of 250 or so tier-3 functions for the whole enterprise.

All of the functions they describe will be valid, of course, but most will be tier-4 'tasks' which can be listed in the supporting document. What you're after here is the small handful of – to them – higher-level tier-3 functions that summarise their work in relation to everyone else: probably no more than half a dozen functions each, in practice.

Do remember, though, to document any tier-4 functions you come across: they'll be important for end-to-end process-design and information-mapping at later stages in the enterprise-architecture.

Application themes: tier-4 functions

For each tier-3 activity:

- What are the tasks within the activity?
- How do these functions relate with each other, in terms of service-categories and service-layering?

Unlike the other tiers, which are usually rather more abstract collations or aggregations of business-functions, tier-4 'tasks' will either be, or be close to, actual tangible work. Since they don't have to be squeezed onto the diagram, there can be any number of these: document them in any way that seems appropriate to the business need.

Verifying a Function Model

As the model is developed, it needs to be verified for completeness. The simplest way to do this is to think of each function as a service, with each component intimately interlinked with and dependent on all of the other services within the enterprise, and (certainly at tier-3 and above) containing other subsidiary services which it coordinates to deliver its overall 'product' – whatever that may be. In effect, the whole enterprise delivers one or more services to its clients, and in turn 'consumes' services from other entities such as suppliers, partners, government and other stakeholders.

To verify 'completeness' in a viable-services sense, the essential test is that each of the Viable System Model 'systems' is present in some form or other – either 'contained' within the respective service, or provided via a link from some other service. In addition to routine audit in the specific terms for that service, it's also advisable to verify that quality-management of some kind is applied consistently throughout the enterprise, as a mandatory pervasive-service for every context. The checklist that follows addresses all of these concerns, but in practice is only the minimum check that should be applied: add further context-specific tests to the list as appropriate.

Application themes: verifying a Function Model

Apply the following checklist to each function, and at each tier:

- **policy**: what is the service's *purpose*? who or what defines *policy*?
- **strategy**: what is the current *strategy*? outside *relationships*? who defines this?
- **manage**: how are the service's *tasks defined*, *managed* and *monitored*?
- **verify**: what random checks or *audits* are used to *verify* performance?
- **coordinate**: how is the service *coordinated* with other services?
- **tasks**: what does the service *do*? how does it do it? how does it support its 'downline' services (if any)?
- **exceptions**: how does the service identify and resolve any *run-time exceptions*?
- **quality**: what *corrective-action* does the service undertake for *causes* of issues?

- **track**: how does the service *track* and manage *quality-issues* and other issues?
- **improve**: how does the service manage *improvement* of its *processes*?

Each of these checklist-items should reference services that this function 'consumes', either from other functions, or from subsidiary functions and tasks within itself. In principle, every one of these services must exist *somewhere* – otherwise the organisation would be unable to operate.

> Or operate *well*, at any rate: hence the notion of a 'viable service'. A key part of 'to-be' functional design is to identify support-relationships for services that the function does not contain within itself. Serious viability problems can occur if those support-links are either missing or poorly-maintained – the absence of explicit support for corrective-action and quality-management being classic examples that I've seen in all too many business-environments.

Document any identified gaps, and resolve these gaps wherever practicable.

In many cases, the required support-services or links will in fact exist, but are not recognised as such: they may be implied in what is actually done in practice, but no explicit formal procedures exist to call for them. In others, the links might be subsumed under a generic task-heading of 'responsibilities of line-management' or suchlike – but there may be no explicit means to ensure that the work required within the respective service-interrelationship is actually done.

And in some cases, the links may be erratic, or entirely absent, often with results whose symptoms are all too obvious, but whose cause is not. High-pressure production environments, for example, are notorious for losing track of any future-focussed business-purpose, or of failing to understand the crucial quality-management distinction between 'correction' – "fix it up to get the job out of the door" – versus 'corrective action' – "make sure it doesn't happen again". All of these concerns – most often from inadequate integration of pervasive-services – need to be resolved before the enterprise can become fully viable, and fully alive.

Function Model examples

Two examples of completed function-models follow.

The first example is described below as for a 'plastics factory' – actually adapted from the function-model for one division of an organisation in another industry, de-identified and re-captioned to preserve commercial confidentiality. This shows the relatively simple case of an enterprise with a single straight-through value-chain, from customer-order – in most cases received via another division of the organisation, hence only minimally addressed here – through to transfer to fulfilment-processes, which were again handled by another division.

Functions: manufacturing division of (fictional) plastics firm

The organisation had several distributed work-sites, hence inter-site transport was an important factor. The zone shown above the main value-chain provides the policy and strategy management-services and, to some extent, the pervasive-services; the zone below the 'transport' function shows typical support-services provided by central management.

The second example is adapted from an early version of a model developed for a *state-government department* in the social-services sector. This is considerably more complex than the previous example, because it has separate value-streams for each of its five distinct 'services to citizens', plus an additional value-stream for its formal relations with government and its many other societal stakeholders.

All value-streams share many of the same support-services, which makes it inappropriate to use a simple layout of straight-through value-chains, as in the previous example. Instead, a two-tier Viable System Model layout is used, with the main delivery-services shown above as one of the tiers, and the support-services shown below as the other.

Functions: government department in social-services sector

The same vertical axis is used in both tiers, other than that the 'Channel' (customer) row is not used in the second tier, because the customer-facing delivery-services are implicitly 'customers' for the support-services. The categories in the vertical axis are:

- *channel* – delivery-services (customer-facing only)
- *deliver* – delivery-services
- *fund to deliver* – delivery-services
- *educate and train* – delivery-services
- *coordinate* – 'direction' management-services, 'run the business' coordination-services
- *monitor and improve* – pervasive services, 'change the business' coordination-services
- *research, prepare, plan* – 'policy' and 'strategy' management-services, 'develop the business' coordination-services

Some of the apparent gaps are intentional – for example, some value-streams do not deliver community-education services, and others do not provide internal training. Other gaps, though, are genuine, indicating potential or actual problems for the enterprise.

Resources

📖 Function-model examples: see Tom Graves, 'The Viable Services Model: Service quality, service interdependence and service completeness' in Jan van Bon [ed.], *IT Service Management: Global best practices* (itSMF/Van Haren, 2008)

📖 Requirements-gathering (as an analogue for gathering information on business-functions): see Suzanne Robertson and James Robertson, *Mastering the Requirements Process* (Addison-Wesley, 1999)

🕸 Enhanced Telecom Operations Map (eTOM): see www.tmforum.org/browse.aspx?catid=1647 and Wikipedia summary at en.wikipedia.org/wiki/ETOM

🕸 Supply-Chain Operations Reference-model (SCOR): see www.supply-chain.org/cs/root/scor_tools_resources/scor_model/scor_model and Wikipedia summary at en.wikipedia.org/wiki/Supply-Chain_Operations_Reference

PRACTICE – THE KNOWLEDGE OF SERVICES

Summary

With an appropriate Function Model in place, we can cross-link other concerns onto that standard reference-map: these might include information, information-flows, costings, projects, assets, applications, business risks, and much else besides. Such cross-references between the domains create new options for whole-of-enterprise optimisation.

Details

Services and business-systems

Services exchange information; services *are* information. Their structure and design determine the information that needs to flow around the entire enterprise, so that it can deliver its service, its Role within its shared business-context.

Developing the Function Model – as a model of the enterprise in terms of its business functions – is a key step in establishing a service-oriented view of enterprise information, because we can use it as a base on which to build a variety of overlays which have high value in the architecture of the enterprise. One of these is the Business Systems Model.

The purpose of the model is to identify groups of activities that perform the same kinds of functions and are likely to share the same kinds of information, and hence should be supported by similar information-systems. One of the practical aims of this is to ensure that the computer-systems that are developed or purchased to manage this information do not overlap in functionality or in the information that they store.

> Even though this is primarily about information-management, the term 'systems' here is more in the Viable System Model sense, rather than just IT-systems. Remember that much of the core information of an enterprise is word-of-mouth, or individual or collective memory, or built into work-instructions for machines and the like: IT plays an important part in all of this, of course, but it's by no means the only

113

part. Whenever we look at 'information systems', remember also to think of information in the broadest, generic terms – not just the subset of information that's in computer networks and databases.

The simplest way to do this is by using colour-coding for the tier-3 activities on the Function Model. Each colour-code represents a different 'business system', or clustering of related activities. For example, we could split some of the business-systems by service-category-type:

- Is the information about 'develop the business', 'change the business' or 'run the business'?
- Is it about a specific category of delivery-service?
- Is it about funding, or people-management, or customer-relationships?

And so on, and so on. The most appropriate split will depend on the nature of the enterprise – the service delivered by the enterprise as a whole – so there are no straightforward guidelines, but aim to identify some ten to twenty distinct shared areas of information. The resultant set of models would consist of the colour-coded Function-Model diagram and a set of detailed diagrams, for each of the business systems, together with an appropriate textual description.

Application themes: identifying business-systems

- Which tier-3 activities, whether in the same part or different parts of the enterprise, have similar functions and share much the same information?
- What IT-systems or other information-systems would or – for 'to-be' – should these activities use? In IT terms, what applications are or should be used to store and access this information?
- As a cross-check, what existing business-information, information-systems or applications do *not* seem to be used by any activity on the Function Model? What changes would this suggest to the Function Model itself?

We then run the whole process backwards as a further cross-check. For each business system, we need to review the business activities, to verify the 'chunks' of IT functions and the like that would be required to support those business activities. This leads us towards definition of an Information Systems Model, in which these chunks of functionality and related storage are 'information systems' in an abstract sense: they are 'logical' in that they don't describe any specific IT application, for example, but do describe in broad terms what the IT and other applications should do.

We define the information systems at the whole-of-enterprise level, and *without reference to existing IT applications*. This ensures that, overall, the systems and activities each perform functions that make sense to perform together; that there are no overlaps in functionality; and that all of the required functionality is covered. The resultant Information Systems Model consists of an overview diagram or 'context diagram' and a set of more detailed diagrams for each of the 'information systems', together with a textual explanation of the content and role of each system.

At the end of this process, each business-system should be aligned with precisely *one* information-system: there would usually be a variety of applications that might draw on and manipulate that information, but preferably a *single* shared data-store in each case. That's certainly the ideal for any 'to-be' design, though it may not work out that way in practice – especially not in the 'as-is' setup. But what we're really aiming for here is that for each business-system, there is just one 'database of record': a *single source of truth*, in the information sense of the term.

Application themes: identifying single-source-of-truth

For each identified business-system and its information-system:

- What are the sources for transaction-data for this system?
- Who or what may create, read, update or delete transaction-records for this system? For what purposes?
- Who or what may collate transaction-records into aggregations or transformations such as counts-of, trends-of, averages-of and suchlike? For what purposes? Via what transform-processes? Where and in what systems are such transforms maintained? Who or what may create, read, update or delete these transforms, or the means by which the transforms take place?
- What audit-trails exist for changes and aggregations of transaction-data for this system?
- What services do each information-item provide or support?
- Is there a 'single source of truth' for information in this system? If not, what are the consequences of having more than one source of truth?

Reassess the information-systems, the business-systems, and all the way back to the Function Model, in the light of the results of this review.

The value of services

The next step is to use services as a way to map value for the enterprise, in terms of cost, of returns or whatever. The Function Model provides an index into the activities of the enterprise: by mapping any set of values onto the model, we gain a picture of the enterprise in relation to that type of value.

Typical costings-information for this kind of map might include:

- capital expenditure
- operational expenditure
- activity-based costing
- assets-valuation
- investment-valuation

Other options might include financial return – the classic 'return on investment'. Note, though, that even in a commercial organisation, monetary profit may not be the most important value to track here: the most effective core-values to be monitored are those that are linked to enterprise Vision, and which are managed via the pervasive-services rather than solely through the financial accounting-systems.

And other cross-maps that are likely to be useful for whole-of-enterprise optimisation include:

- activities directly or indirectly affected by projects
- activities directly or indirectly affected by changes to legislation or regulation
- activities using specific applications or other assets
- activities in specific geographies or assigned to specific business units

> The value to be gained from these cross-maps depends most on the level of granularity – in other words, how far down into the tiers of the Function Model. A cross-map that stops at tier-1 is unlikely to tell you anything that you don't already know; but going all the way down to tier-4 tasks is probably going to be prohibitively expensive in time and effort – assuming you already have consistent task-mapping across the whole enterprise, which itself is too expensive for all but the most bureaucratic of organisations. If you already have the information to hand, do use it; if not, the usual 'keep it simple' rule applies!

Our experience is that most trade-offs end up somewhere between tier-2 and tier-3. For valuation-maps the cost of collecting the information starts to be prohibitive beyond tier-2 unless the accounting-systems are already set up to support it, but the map is useful even at that relatively coarse granularity. For project cross-maps, though, you really do need to go down to tier-3, to enable the cross-links to the Business Systems Model and Information Systems Model, which are likely to be important, if not essential, in describing impact of projects across the whole enterprise context.

Application themes: Function-Model overlays

- What costings-information or other valuations do you have that can be mapped onto the Function Model? What does such a map show you about the relative cost or value of each activity, at each tier of the Function Model?
- Map current or future projects onto the respective activities on the Function Model, and cross-reference this to the costings maps: what does this tell you about relative targeting of project investment versus activity value? What project overlaps – if any – are highlighted by this cross-map? Which activities are *not* covered by any change-programmes?

These cross-maps will usually highlight architecture- or project-issues that need to be addressed. This is especially true in the early stages of a shift towards a service-oriented enterprise, so don't be surprised at this: just tackle the issues as they arise.

A warning that some of these cross-maps can be embarrassing in a business sense – even scary, sometimes. In one enterprise, for example, we found that we had half a dozen projects, with a total cost of some twenty million dollars, all tackling one area of business that was worth barely a tenth of that, whilst the highest-value aspects of the business received no attention at all. As usual, the culprit there was inappropriate IT-centrism – doing IT 'solutions' for the sake of it, without awareness of its impact on *overall* performance. In another case, in a logistics environment, we found that we had three distinct projects, each requiring separate but incompatible RFID radio-tracking infrastructures, all demanding to take exclusive control of the same physical space: no-one had previously thought to check. Ouch…

In yet another case, though, an odd gap in coverage pointed to the unexpected merits of a small, unimportant-seeming project that had previously been turned down twice as having no apparent business-case. On its own, it didn't: but the cross-map showed that it would act as the linch-pin for half a dozen other major projects, greatly increasing *their* overall value to the enterprise. Once we'd explained that to the executive, the project gained its go-ahead in a hurry.

> Embarrassing or not, such matters are important in optimising the ability of the enterprise to deliver its services. And as enterprise-architects, that's what we're here to do: this is part of how we get good at doing it!

One of the main ways we can do this is to use service-architecture concepts as a guide: for each area of impact, what are the delivery-services, the management-services? What coordination between services would be required? What values need to be supported and monitored in each context, via what pervasive-services? Once we establish that as a review-pattern for each of these cross-maps, the service-oriented enterprise tends almost to create itself.

Verifying viability

Another use of the Function Model is as a means to verify viability of all services across the enterprise. To do this, we use much the same process and checklist as when verifying the validity of the overall model (see p.108); but this time it's not just about confirming that the required links exist, but more about validating the viability of each of the links themselves.

The key theme here is that each entity on the Function Model is, in effect, a reference to the 'direction' management-service for that service. The relationships between the 'direction' service and other categories and sub-types of services in the viable-services model indicate the links that need to be in place *somewhere* to support the respective 'direction'-service. Sometimes the required links are internal to the activity, but often they're not, and that's what we aim to identify here.

Application themes: viable relations

For each tier-3 activity:

- Who or what provides 'policy' management-services for this activity? If it exists, is it internal or external to the activity? If external, is it spread across more than one other activity?
- Who or what provides 'strategy' management-services for this activity? If it exists, is it internal or external to the activity? If external, is it spread across more than one other activity?
- Who or what provides 'develop the business' coordination-services for this activity? If it exists, is it internal or external to the activity? If external, is it spread across more than one other activity? With what other services does it coordinate these tasks?

118

- Who or what provides 'change the business' coordination-services for this activity? If it exists, is it internal or external to the activity? If external, is it spread across more than one other activity? With what other services does it coordinate these tasks?

- Who or what provides 'run the business' coordination-services for this activity? If it exists, is it internal or external to the activity? If external, is it spread across more than one other activity? With what other services does it coordinate these tasks?

- Who or what acts as the 'parent' delivery-service for this activity? In what ways does the parent coordinate resources for this and its other 'child'-activities? What performance-information needs to be passed to the parent for this purpose? If other information is passed 'upward' or 'downward' with the parent for other purposes, what information, and for what purposes?

- Who or what acts as the 'child' delivery-services – if any – for this activity? In what ways does this activity coordinate resources for its 'child'-activities? What performance-information needs to be garnered from the 'child'-activities for this for this purpose? If other information is passed 'upward' or 'downward' with the children for other purposes, what information, and for what purposes?

- Who or what provides 'run the business' coordination-services for the 'child'-tasks (if any) of this activity? If it exists, is it internal or external to the activity? If external, is it spread across more than one other activity? With what other services does it coordinate these tasks?

- For each enterprise value, who or what provides 'develop awareness' pervasive-services for that value in this activity? Who or what provides 'develop capability' pervasive-services for that value in this activity? Who or what provides 'audit' pervasive-services for that value in this activity? If each exists, is it internal or external to the activity? If external, is it spread across more than one other activity? How do these link back to the core values of the enterprise?

In effect, this also provides the content for a RACI matrix for each activity:

- *responsible* or 'accountable' – the business-owner of the activity (there should be exactly one person – not just role, but real person – with this assignment for each activity)
- *assists* – those who assist the responsible person in the overall work of the activity
- *consulted* – those whose opinions may be sought concerning the activity (two-way communication)
- *informed* – those who need to be kept up-to-date on changes concerning the activity (one-way communication)

In RACI terms, the links identified in the review above point to activities with an 'assists'-relationship to the respective activity. In effect, each of these is a stakeholder in the activity – which means that each link will also point to people who will often need to be consulted, and at the least informed, about any changes to the activity. So in addition to identifying mutual cross-dependencies, this also creates a map of mutual responsibilities across the entire enterprise.

The next stage is to map the *content* of each of these links, which in turn points to the required *structure* – and hence the appropriate types of implementation for each link.

Application themes: viable communications

For each link to and from each tier-3 activity:

- What *physical* resources and other items would be transferred across the link? By what means should these items be transferred? What storage-measures, security-measures and other qualitative concerns should apply to such transfers?
- What information and other *virtual* assets should be exchanged across the link? By what means should these items be exchanged? What storage-measures, security-measures and other qualitative concerns should apply to each exchange?
- What interpersonal connections and other *relational* issues apply to each link? By what means should these connections be established and maintained? What security-measures and other qualitative concerns should apply to each connection?
- What purpose and other *aspirational* concerns apply to each link? By what means should these concerns be established and verified? What security-measures and other qualitative themes should apply to each of these concerns?

120

- What other *abstract* concerns such as time, finance and funding would apply across the link? By what means should these concerns be identified, applied and verified? What security-measures and other qualitative themes should apply to each of these concerns?

This review provides a model not just of existing structures and services, but also of any 'missing' capabilities that would need to exist in order to support viability across the enterprise. In that sense, it amplifies our *knowledge* of the enterprise and its services.

All of this is valuable from an IT perspective, because it identifies content and structure for the Information Systems Model, and the IT-systems and applications that would be needed to support it. But we do need to be thinking wider than just IT-style 'service-oriented architecture': these are the transactions across the *whole* of the service-oriented enterprise, not just its IT – and we may need to implement those exchanges and transactions in many different ways.

Resources

⬟ Activity-Based Costing: see Wikipedia summary at en.wikipedia.org/wiki/Activity-based_costing

📖 Viable System Model in organisation design: see Patrick Hoverstadt, *The Fractal Organization: Creating sustainable organizations with the Viable System Model* (Wiley, 2008)

PRACTICE – SERVICES IN ACTION

Summary

The practical purpose of a service is to get something done – it *delivers* a service of some kind to the customer or consumer of that service. Practical concerns that arise from this include the need to ask what the service does, how it does so, and how the various functions and services are coordinated into a seamless business-process that provides the final service that the customer receives.

Details

Actions and transactions

On their own, services do nothing. To be useful – to contribute to the overall service of the enterprise – they need to be linked to other services in a choreographed sequence of transactions, as a *business process*. So it's here that we turn to the standard process-modelling tools and techniques, in order to describe the run-time relationships between services, and the choreography mechanisms that link them together into a business-process.

So let's take a (much-simplified) example of a service to create a new account, as described in the standard BPMN (Business Process Modelling Notation) format:

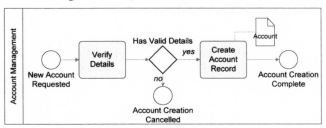

Simplified content of encapsulated service 'Create Account'

This identifies and describes the following components:

- the overall service, and responsibility for the service, indicated by the enclosing 'swimlane' rectangle and its descriptive label

- the start, end and exception-end events, represented by circles
- calls to two child-services, represented by rounded-rectangles
- a decision – part of the internal choreography – represented by a diamond
- an artefact of some kind for the resultant account, represented by a folded-paper symbol
- the sequence of interactions, represented by the connecting lines

> For this example, don't worry too much about details of layout or content or suchlike. We could just as well describe it in the form of a UML (Unified Modelling Language) process-diagram, or any other process-modelling notation: the presentation would differ somewhat, of course, but the principles would be much the same. The specific form or representation doesn't much matter here: it's the *principles* we're concerned with – the modelling of service *as* service.

But notice also what is *not* described in the model:

- no indication as to *how* the service is implemented, or what form the account-artefact should take
- no indication as to what happens before the start-event or after either of the end-events, or what information or other resources are transferred to or from the service on those events
- no indication of what information and other resources are used within the service
- no indication of what information and other resources are referenced but not consumed within the service
- no indication of what performance-metrics should be provided by the service, or to which other services they should be provided

Many of those concerns would be addressed in a more detailed model – particularly about any information and other artefacts to be transferred to and from the service. There *is* a definite problem in both BPMN and UML, in that both assume that any resources will always be virtual – hence BPMN's term 'Data Object' for what should really be a generic artefact – and that both at least imply that execution would always be via IT. But in fact there's no reason to assume an IT-only implementation: the service in that example could just as well be delivered by an entirely manual, paper-based process, or even by a machine-based one in some industrial contexts: the fact that implementation is not predefined isn't a mistake, it's a *necessary* requirement for all 'logical'-layer modelling.

More relevant here, perhaps, is that there are no assumptions about how the 'child' sub-processes are to be implemented. They might indeed be handled by 'child' delivery-services; they might instead be inline within this service; the choice doesn't matter much, in principle at least, though there may be practical considerations that could drive the choice one way or the other in different implementations.

More worrying is that there really is no built-in means in either of those modelling-notations to enforce support for those essential performance-metrics. There's also very little acknowledgement of how the choreography and coordination-processes would actually happen. That's a typical consequence of the machine-metaphor, in which choreography is presumed to be a 'brain' function from outside of 'the machine' itself; but it's an oversight that causes real difficulties when translating a BPMN model even into a form suitable for IT execution, let alone for anything else.

In practice, these things *matter*: we need to be ready for them in designing viable services. Even if the internal service-execution is much the same, a process that needs different performance-metrics or different control-artefacts may well need support from a different service.

Application themes: process-choreography – processes

For each business-process:

- Which services link other services together into the choreography of this business-process? Through what mechanisms does that choreography occur? What service-contracts apply to the choreography *as* a service in itself?
- What signals – synchronous, asynchronous, whatever – are in use to ensure that processes happen in the right sequence, at the right times and in response to the right events? What form do these signals take?
- What mechanisms are used to handle exceptions in the execution of the process? To which services are any exceptions passed, and what types of exceptions in each case? What actions must be taken once the exception is passed?
- What resources are needed for this coordination-service to operate? Via which management-services does it obtain the required resources?

- What performance-metrics does it collate, from individual services within the process-choreography, and from within itself? To what management-services does it pass these performance-metrics?
- What management-services define policy and strategy for this choreography-service?
- What, if any, are the 'child'-services for this service?
- Which coordination-services provide 'develop the business', 'change the business' and 'run the business' support for this service?
- Which pervasive-services guide and audit compliance with quality-concerns and other enterprise-values for this service?

Application themes: process-choreography – services

For each service in the business-process:

- What interfaces are exposed for choreography-services to discover? Via what mechanisms may the choreography-process discover that interface? Via what mechanisms may the choreography-process identify that the service is available for transactions? Through what mechanisms may a transaction occur? What service-contracts apply to the transactions?
- What mechanisms are used to handle exceptions in the internal execution of the service? Via what mechanisms are any exceptions notified to the connecting choreography-process, and what types of exceptions in each case? What rollback and other actions must be taken by the service once the exception has been passed?
- What resources are needed for this service to operate in different process-choreographies? Via which management-services does it obtain the required resources?
- What performance-metrics does the service collate regarding its transactions in service-choreographies, from within itself, and from any 'child'-services? To what management-services does it pass these performance-metrics?
- What management-services define policy and strategy for the use of this service in process-choreographies?
- Which coordination-services provide 'develop the business', 'change the business' and 'run the business' support for the use of this service in process-choreographies?

- Which pervasive-services guide and audit compliance with quality-concerns and other enterprise-values for when this service is used in process-choreography by 'external' services?

This may seem like a lot to assess, but none of it is trivial. One of the most common problems in IT-centric contexts is that whilst the IT-execution is usually excellent, the handling of any non-IT matters will often range from poor to abysmal to non-existent. Everything non-IT gets shoved into the 'too-hard basket', and then promptly forgotten, with disastrous consequences that sooner or later will hit home very hard indeed. Formal service-management processes such as ITIL (IT Infrastructure Library) will help, but tend to be at too high a granularity: they deal with the human side of IT-management, but not so much with the handovers between IT and everything else in the detail of run-time processes – and the latter is where everything tends to fall over. It's that detail that we aim to address in reviews such as those above.

Breaking free from IT

IT-centrism is probably *the* single greatest problem at present for service-oriented architectures. A service is a service: the choice of mechanism by which it's implemented should always be a secondary concern relative to the structure and role of the service itself. But the obsessive IT-centrism of the present means that the architecture process ends up being run backward: we start with some IT-based capability, then look for services to implement with it – and any services that can't be implemented by IT are ignored as 'out of scope', which inevitably results in process-gaps that are 'invisible' *because* they're not amenable to implementation by IT. In short, a guaranteed recipe for disaster – which is exactly what we see in all too many would-be service-architectures.

Application themes: challenging IT-centrism

- What tendencies do you see in your own enterprise towards IT-centrism – the implicit assumption not only that every problem has an IT-based solution, but that the latest style of IT-based solutions will always be inherently *better* than any other option?
- In what ways is such IT-centrism reflected in the enterprise-architecture?
- What are the consequences of such IT-centrism? For example, what clashes arise as a result between IT and the rest of the

business? And what could you do within the enterprise-architecture to defuse some of these clashes?

The core of the problem is actually a side-effect of IT's own success. It's so well suited to managing all manner of rule-based contexts that it's easy to believe that IT would excel at handling *everything* – which it doesn't. In particular, it is *not* good with true complexity. And unfortunately, whether we like it or not, much of the real world *is* complex – which means straight away that every rule-based system is likely to fail in unexpected ways.

In effect, IT-centrism is a kind of last-gasp version of the machine-metaphor, the assumption that the world 'ought to be' predictable in the ways that we want and expect, so that everything can be 'under control' at all times. Whenever IT-centrism meets the real world, there's always a reflex attempt to force the world to fit the constraints of its rule-based logic, and then complain that the world is somehow being unfair when it doesn't conform to those expectations. The psychology of all this is kind of interesting… but it doesn't help all that much. What *does* help is being clear about what IT is good at, and what it isn't, and using each approach appropriately. There's a kind of gradation here:

- *rule-based*: no choice or judgement permitted, little to no true skill; real-time or near-real-time only, and strictly causal; may be implemented by machines, IT or people
- *analytic*: some judgement required, with choices amongst complicated paths, sometimes with delays and disconnects in time, but modelled in terms of cause-effect relationships; usually cannot be implemented by machines without IT-based or human support
- *heuristic*: true skills and judgement always required, to assess contextual patterns with high uncertainties, limited statistical probabilities, complex delays and unknown or unidentified factors; apparent patterns of cause-effect identified only retrospectively; cannot be implemented by machines or conventional IT-based systems without human support
- *principle-based*: very high skill-levels, extreme and inherent uncertainty in real-time or near-real-time; no direct cause-effect patterns identifiable (e.g. 'market of one'); can only be implemented by humans

The further we move away from a simple rule-based context, the more expensive the IT becomes; and whenever there's a shift to true complexity, the IT is usually so costly, unreliable, inefficient, or any such, that there *must* be a way to hand over to a 'manual' version of the process. If there isn't a way to escalate an exception up to a human decision, a people-based means to provide the *same* nominal service, that service will eventually fail. It's as simple as that. So we need to design for that from the beginning – *not* just as an afterthought.

> One of our government clients gave us an example of this, which for them had proved embarrassing in the extreme. Newspaper headlines yet again about apparent failures at the department: a Category One incident must be resolved within a single day, thundered the editorial, yet here were *ten* Category Ones in *one suburb* that still hadn't been closed off in *more than a month*. What's gone wrong *this* time?
>
> Nothing much, in reality. It was indeed true that there were ten distinct reports, and it was also true that they still hadn't been cleared after more than a month. Yet in fact they all related to the same single incident, concerning an unborn child, which had indeed been fully resolved within a matter of a few hours. But they couldn't link the reports together until they had a database record for the child; and they couldn't create that record because the key-field was date-of-birth – and the child hadn't been born yet. No manual override, hence no way to mark the incident as cleared – and hence a field-day for the first investigative journalist who happened to glance at the statistics published on the department's own website. Oops...
>
> Moral of this story: if you don't want to appear as your local equivalent of bad headlines in the newspaper, make sure that every single one of your services allows some means to do a manual override...

Note that this occurs not just with decisions about information, but with physical skills too: each new generation of machinery has been created by someone with a high degree of skill pushing the technology beyond its normal limitations.

The same applies to the relational dimension of business. As many banks have discovered the hard way, there are indeed limits as to how many types of transactions customers are willing to do only through ATMs and other IT: at some point they will *need* to talk with a real person, if only to resolve some exception that the IT can't handle – or has created in the first place. Service-oriented architecture is not just about the detail-level IT, but is ultimately about *service* – in every sense of that term.

So we need to extend SOA beyond IT, to the *whole* of the enterprise. Yet we should still aim to use the same core principles as described for IT-based SOA back in *Basics – Service-oriented architecture* (see p11):

- loosely-coupled

128

- contract-based
- discoverable
- abstraction and encapsulation
- reusable and recomposable
- interchangeable with equivalent services

To illustrate this, we could take an example of services at almost the opposite extreme from IT-SOA, but still recognisable to and relevant for enterprise-architects: a free-form consortium of consultants:

- Each consultant in the consortium presents a *service* – each has specific skills and experience to offer.
- A business-process such as strategy might call on any number of these consultants, in any order: in that sense, the interface would be *loosely-coupled*.
- There would need to be some kind of *contract*-relationship, whether formal or informal.
- The consultants and their services would need to be *discoverable*, with identifiable interfaces – if only in the form of email-addresses and the like.
- We know what kind of results we want from the consultants, but how they do that work would be largely up to them: in that sense, there's *abstraction* and *encapsulation*.
- We might use the consultants in almost any order, and in many different tasks and processes: their services are *reusable, recomposable* and, to some extent, *interchangeable*.

So it all fits: the same architecture principles apply. But what else needs to happen, architecturally speaking, to make this kind of service-oriented consortium a reality? We can use the same review-process as before to explore this service-context, with each usage of the consortium as a business-process in its own right, each with its own choreographed sequence of connections and contextual transactions.

Application themes: consultancy as service

For each business-process that uses the consortium:

- Which services link the consortium's services together into the choreography of this business-process? Through what mechanisms does that choreography occur? What service-contracts apply to the choreography as a service in itself?

- What signals – synchronous, asynchronous, whatever – are in use to ensure that the services of the different consultants are called for in the right sequence, at the right times and in response to the right events? What form do these signals take?
- What mechanisms are used to handle exceptions in the execution of the process? To which services are any exceptions passed, and what types of exceptions in each case? What actions must be taken once the exception is passed?
- What resources are needed for this coordination-service to operate? Via which management-services does it obtain the required resources?
- What performance-metrics does it collate, from individual services within the process-choreography, and from within itself? To what management-services does it pass these performance-metrics?
- What management-services define policy and strategy for this choreography-service?
- What, if any, are the 'child'-services for this choreography-service?
- Which coordination-services provide 'develop the business', 'change the business' and 'run the business' support for this consortium *as* a service?
- Which pervasive-services guide and audit compliance with quality-concerns and other enterprise-values for the overall services of the consortium?

For each service in the business-process – each member of the consultants' consortium:

- What interfaces are exposed for choreography-services to discover? Via what mechanisms may a choreography-process discover that interface? Via what mechanisms may the choreography-process identify that the service is available for transactions? Through what mechanisms may a transaction occur? What service-contracts apply to the transactions? What forms would those interfaces and transactions take? And what artefacts would be transferred in either direction as part of each transaction?
- What mechanisms are used to handle exceptions in the internal execution of the service? Via what mechanisms are any exceptions notified to the connecting choreography-process, and what types of exceptions in each case? What

rollback and other actions must be taken by the service once the exception has been passed?

- What resources are needed for this service to operate in different process-choreographies? Via which management-services does it obtain the required resources?
- What performance-metrics does the service collate regarding its transactions in service-choreographies, from within itself, and from any 'child'-services? To what management-services does it pass these performance-metrics?
- What management-services define policy and strategy for the use of this service in the consortium's process-choreography?
- Which coordination-services provide 'develop the business', 'change the business' and 'run the business' support for the use of this service in the consortium's choreographies?
- Which pervasive-services guide and audit compliance with quality-concerns and other enterprise-values for when this service is used in process-choreography by 'external' services? What *are* the enterprise Vision, values, policies, regulations and other pervasive themes for the consortium?

At first glance this may seem a lot more complex than for something like a simple web-service setup. Yet whilst it's true that the context being managed by the consortium may be quite a bit more difficult to define, with interfaces that tend to be much more free-form in nature, the exact same principles do apply in both cases

It's not that the consortium is inherently more difficult to design: it's more that IT service-designers tend to leave out half of that list from their analyses, with unfortunate consequences such as those we've seen earlier. Service-oriented architecture can be applied to any context; and should apply in the same ways throughout *every* aspect of the service-oriented enterprise.

Resources

- Business Process Modelling Notation (BPMN): see www.bpmn.org and Wikipedia summary at en.wikipedia.org/wiki/BPMN
- Unified Modelling Language (UML): see www.uml.org and Wikipedia summary at en.wikipedia.org/wiki/Unified_Modeling_Language
- IT Infrastructure Library (ITIL) for IT service-management: see www.itil-officialsite.com

⬟ Service-oriented IT-architecture: see Wikipedia summary at en.wikipedia.org/wiki/Service_oriented_architecture

📖 Breaking free from IT-centric assumptions in enterprise-architecture: see Tom Graves, *Real Enterprise Architecture: beyond IT to the whole enterprise* (Tetradian, 2008) and Tom Graves, *Bridging the Silos: enterprise architecture for IT-architects* (Tetradian, 2008)

PRACTICE – OPTIMISING SERVICES

Summary

From the customer's perspective, the service ends once the results specified in the service-contract have been delivered. But for the service-provider, there's a need for a final phase to review what has been done, and how well it has been done – and what else could be done to improve the overall effectiveness of the service-oriented enterprise.

Details

Audit and improvement

Another of the architectural concerns arising from a technology-centred approach to service-architecture is that almost all of the attention is on service-execution and service-choreography, with little left over to assess what happens next. The service may be complete at that point from the requester's perspective, but not to the service-provider: there's still a fair amount of work that needs to be done after the nominal service-request ends.

First of these is the provision of the service-performance records required by the parent management-service: they may not seem relevant to the service itself, but they *are* indeed needed for overall resource-management and service-coordination. And then later – sometimes quite a lot later – there will need to be an audit, to verify the performance-information coming up the hierarchy-tree. More accurately, there needs to be at least one audit-process for *each* of the core-values of the enterprise – and performance-metrics to match, too.

If those audits don't take place, there's almost no point in defining the respective values, because there would be no way to ensure that the enterprise is 'on track' towards its vision, role, missions or goals. And they need to pervade *every* part of the enterprise – which means that the audits need to apply to *every* service, all the way down to the manual processes and the detail-level IT.

If we can't measure it, we can't manage it. And if we can't manage it, we can't improve it either. Those audits *matter*.

Application themes: audit to improve

- What audit-processes already exist for the services in your enterprise? What concerns and values are audited, and for what purposes?
- What performance-information is passed up the hierarchy-tree from each service? If this information passes through various transforms and aggregations on its way up the tree, by what means can the original source-information be identified and audited?
- By what architectural means can you ensure that performance-metrics are garnered for *every* enterprise core-value? By what means can you ensure that such information is collected in formats amenable to subsequent audit?
- In what ways is performance-information – as verified via audit – re-used and re-applied in the improvement-processes of the enterprise? In what parts of the enterprise, and for what services, do these respective improvement-processes apply?
- What audit-information and audit-processes are used to verify each instance of intended improvement?
- Where multiple implementations exist for a single service – such as for disaster-recovery or load-balancing – by what means can you ensure that the same overall audit-processes and audit-criteria apply to all implementations?
- What information-gaps and audit-gaps exist in the enterprise? If any, in what areas and at what levels of the enterprise do those gaps occur? What can you do to resolve those gaps, in terms of the service-architecture, service-designs and service implementations?

The audit is also the last stage of the pervasive-services' own improvement-cycle of develop–awareness, develop-capability and audit, which maintain momentum towards an ever-improving expression of the enterprise values. In its way, this is much the same as the Deming/Shewhart quality-improvement cycle of *plan, do, check, act*, with develop-awareness as 'plan', develop-capability as 'do', the audit itself as 'check', and the follow-up to the audit as 'act'. So there needs to be quite a strong cross-reference between the pervasive-services and the 'change the business' coordination-services that guide the planned changes to the service-catalogue, the service-choreographies and the services themselves.

Improvement and optimisation

Perhaps the most important part of any improvement-cycle – and the part that turns it into a *cycle*, rather than a linear goal-based sequence – is the 'lessons-learned' process that occurs after all the nominal work is complete. In the TOGAF ADM enterprise architecture methodology, for example, there's a 'Phase H' review-phase that occurs at the end of the architecture-iteration; in the Deming cycle, it's the 'check' phase, leading to the 'act' analysis that starts a new cycle. One of the simplest yet most effective techniques for this is the US Army's 'After Action Review': which consists of just four questions:

- *"What was supposed to happen?"* – 'plan'
- *"What actually happened?"* – 'do'
- *"What was the source of the difference?"* – 'check'
- *"What can we learn from this, to do different next time?"* – 'act'

The whole review can be done in a matter of minutes. Aim to spend perhaps a quarter of the time on the first two questions, another quarter on the third question, and half the time on the last. There's also one firm rule for the review, called "pin your stripes at the door": regardless of any nominal rank, no-one has priority, everyone is equal – everyone had their job to do, their own responsibilities, and the aim is for *everyone* to find out how to do their work better, both individually and as a collective team.

In a service-architecture context, we might apply much the same principles to review how we model patterns of 'completeness' or 'incompleteness'; the recursion of patterns in service-structures; the trade-offs between abstract services and their real implementations in 'normal' business-processes and for abnormal conditions such as disaster-recovery; or other trade-offs, such as optimisation of service transactions. If each of those is the plan – 'what was supposed to happen?' – then what did the service actually do? What caused the difference between intention, expectation and real-world result? What can we learn from this? That's what this type of review would explore.

The specific content of the review doesn't matter that much here: what *does* matter is that some kind of lessons-learned review must take place immediately after the action is over, and that the results of those reviews should feed back into service-improvement.

Application themes: lessons-learned

- What 'lessons-learned' processes exist for the enterprise-architecture, and for services in general throughout the enterprise?
- What is learned from such reviews? In what ways do you act on the 'lessons learned'?
- By what means do the results of such lessons-learned reviews feed back into the 'change the business' coordination-services? How would you verify that those results have been applied – and applied appropriately – within the change-processes?

Another point here is that this is also a *social* process, in which the context is viewed from multiple levels and multiple perspectives. It's not the machine-metaphor's rigid separation between 'brawn-less brain' and 'brainless brawn': we make full use of experience and knowledge from *every* aspect of the context, to identify and apply those 'lessons learned'. So whilst the architecture for a service-oriented enterprise will involve a great deal of analysis, of *thinking* and suchlike, it's also necessarily a social process of engagement with each of the service's stakeholders. To create the *effectiveness* that we need across the entire enterprise, optimisation depends on that process of engagement.

Optimisation and engagement

An enterprise is a social community, sharing a common purpose. And social communities operate – or literally *co*-operate – through mutual service. So service isn't just some 'nice idea' for academics: it's a key survival-strategy in any unstable ecosystem. Service-orientation *matters*.

If the sense of service is a desirable core-value for the enterprise, and a service-orientation is a desirable outcome for that value, then service-oriented architecture is implicitly is, and needs to be, one of the pervasive-services for the enterprise. Which means that a key part of architecture work must revolve around engaging people in the *practical* expression of the value of services: creating awareness of that value; developing capability to support it; verifying that that value is in real everyday use, guiding decision-making throughout the enterprise; and taking action to enhance it wherever practicable, again throughout the enterprise. A service-oriented architecture doesn't sit in one place, hidden away in the enterprise equivalent of an ivory tower: it's *everywhere*. Engagement *is* the architecture.

Describing the detailed processes needed for architectural engagement would require a book in itself: but fortunately we don't have to do that, because the information we need already exists elsewhere, in practical research on change-management, knowledge-management and so on. Some recommended sources include:

- knowledge-sharing within large organisations, such as described by Collison and Parcell, and many others
- knowledge-sharing through 'communities of practice', such as described by Etienne Wenger and his colleagues
- narrative knowledge and 'business story-telling', such as described by Shawn Callahan and others at the Australian consultancy Anecdote
- developing and sustaining a proactive, self-adapting 'learning organisation', such as described by Peter Senge and colleagues

The knowledge needed for optimisation of services is distributed throughout the enterprise: engagement in architecture is one of the key means by which the enterprise can access that knowledge from within itself.

Application themes: architecture engagement

- What processes and tools do you use to engage stakeholders in the various stages of the architecture process – particularly the review-phases?
- How do you publish and promulgate the results of your work at present? What architecture artefacts do you produce?
- What mechanisms exist to garner and incorporate feedback into the architecture? What can you do to make that happen, and to verify the quality of what happens?
- What support does your existing architecture-toolset provide in this? If any exists, is it broadcast-only, does it allow feedback via annotation, or is it fully bidirectional?
- How do you measure the effectiveness of architecture? How is the business-value of the architecture itself identified and measured? What metrics are used for this? What improvements could be made in those metrics, and in the ways in which they are gathered, reviewed and re-used?
- What metrics are used to measure the value of the overall enterprise? In what terms are those metrics defined? To what extent do they align with the espoused vision and values of the enterprise? If the alignment is poor, what could you do in architectural terms to improve it?

- What else could you do to enhance awareness and engagement by the enterprise in its own architecture?

In the end, the real driver here – the real 'desirable value' – is to improve enterprise *effectiveness*: improved efficiency, reliability, clarity and simplicity, everything 'on purpose', everything and everyone working together towards the common aims. Service-oriented architecture and an overall service-orientation for the enterprise will definitely help in this endeavour. As an enterprise architect, how much of that ideal may be fulfilled is ultimately up to you.

Resources

🏯 Deming/Shewhart 'Plan, Do, Check, Act' cycle: see Wikipedia summary at en.wikipedia.org/wiki/PDCA

🏯 TOGAF lessons-learned phase: see www.opengroup.org/architecture/togaf8-doc/arch/toc.html (chapter 'Phase H: Architecture Change Management')

📖 US Army After Action Review as 'lessons learned' in business context, and engagement in knowledge-sharing: see Chris Collison and Geoff Parcell, *Learning to Fly: practical lessons from one of the world's leading knowledge companies* (Capstone, 2001)

📖 Peter Senge et al., *The Dance of Change: the challenges of sustaining momentum in learning organizations* (Nicholas Brealey Publishing, 1999)

🏯 Narrative knowledge and business-storytelling: see www.anecdote.com.au

🏯 Etienne Wenger on 'communities of practice': see www.ewenger.com/theory/

📖 Etienne Wenger, Richard McDermott and William M. Snyder, *Cultivating Communities of Practice: a guide to managing knowledge* (Harvard Business School Press, 2002)

APPENDIX: BUILDING A FUNCTION MODEL IN VISIO

Preliminaries

Unpack the template

Download the template-archive from the Tetradian Books website at tetradianbooks.com/ebook/function-model.zip . Unpack the archive to an appropriate folder on your system.

Copy the stencil-file function-model.vss from the archive-folder to your 'My Documents\My Shapes' folder.

Copy the template-file function-model-tpl.vst from the archive-folder to a templates folder – preferably the folder pointed to by the 'Templates' path in Visio's Tools > Options: Advanced: File Paths dialog.

Application

Create a new function-model file

Double-click on the template function-model-tpl.vst, or – if you've placed the template where Visio can find it – start Visio, click on the menu-item File > New... and select the Function Model template.

Create the function-model

To create a new function, drag the 'Function' object from the stencil onto the drawing.

Double-click on the object to set its properties:

Name: enter a suitable name for the function, according to your preferred style. On a standard tier-3 'Activity' function you have room for three to four lines, or up to about 40-50 characters. The name for a function should always include a verb.

- Warning: **don't** type the name straight onto the function-object – you'll lose the link to the name in the properties-sheet, which is what's used in reports. If you do accidentally overwrite a name, select the function, then the menu-item 'Insert > Field'. From the pick-list shown, select 'Custom Properties' (left column) and 'Name' (central column), then click 'OK'.

Tier: select the tier – usually only 1, 2 or 3, with 3 being the standard 'Activity'-level function.

- *Tier 1*: place these first on the page, or use 'Shape > Send to back' to place it behind other functions. Drag the handles to set the size, and use 'Format > Fill' to set the colour as appropriate.
- *Tier 2*: these will contain clusters of related tier-3 'Activity' functions. It's automatically set to transparent fill, with the label ('Name' property) in bold at the top. Adjust the size as appropriate by dragging the handles.
- *Tier 3*: these are the standard 'Activity'-level functions. It's probably best not to change the size: leaving the size alone makes it easier to align shapes, and there should be enough room for 250-300 Activities.

Source: specify the documents and other sources from where you identified this function – for example, an org-chart entry, a page in the Annual Report, and so on.

Parent: use this in tier-2 and tier-3 functions to identify the 'containing' higher-level function, to help sort entries in reports. Copy the Name property from the properties dialog of the 'parent', then open the properties for each of the 'contained' functions and paste the name into their respective Parent property.

Children: use this in tier-3 Activity functions to identify the list of 'child' tier-4 Tasks within the Activity. It's not required, but it does give you somewhere to record any Tasks that you find, in a way that can be retrieved for a subsequent report.

Bus-system: used only for tier-3 Activity functions, this identifies the 'business system' to which the Activity has been allocated – see *Create a Business Systems model* below.

Description: enter a brief description of the function.

Comments: this is a placeholder for any other comments you may have about the function, such as about its placement in the model.

Add a new page

If you need a new page, select 'Insert > New Page...' from the menu. Fill in appropriate details on the Page Setup dialog.

Warning: a new page should have its business-system properties defined before adding any objects to the page. You will not be able to create a Business Systems model from any functions which were added to the page before this is done. To add the business-system properties:

- ensure that nothing is selected on the new page
- right-click on the page, and select 'Shape > Custom Properties...'
- answer 'Yes' to the 'define custom properties' pop-up
- set the values as follows:
  - label: syslist
  - type: string
  - value: (not defined)
  - prompt: List of business-systems - separate by ';'
- click on the 'New' button, and set the values as follows:
  - label: syscolour
      - note the spelling – British 'colour', not US 'color'
  - type: string
  - value: 1
  - prompt: List of colour-codes for Business Systems - separate by';', in same order as SysList
- click 'OK' to save the custom-properties

It's somewhat of a kludge, but it's the best can be done without adding Visual Basic to the template – which would cause constant annoyances with Microsoft's macro-protection settings.

Create reports

To generate a report, select 'Tools > Reports...' from the menu. Although you can easily create your own report-formats, two standard function-reports are already in the template:

- *function_basic*: Basic function list for general use, showing tier, parent, name, source, description, comments, and sorted by tier, parent and name
- *function_full*: A fuller function-report – more suited for Business System models or output to a final document – which includes tier, parent, name, source, child-tasks, business-system, description, comments, and again sorted by tier, parent and name

Visio will automatically output these to Excel, HTML, XML or another Visio drawing.

Allocate Business Systems

The aim here is to identify a set of fifteen to twenty 'business systems' – clusters of similar Activities in different areas of the business, or related Activities, which share similar or related sets of information – and allocate each Activity to one of these business systems. We do this by colour-coding a copy of the Function-Model, assigning a different colour to each business-system.

Ideally, we should be able to do this automatically: define a colour for each, add an index, and then set the Activity to the respective colour. In Visio, we can do this manually, but it's tedious and error-prone. Although Visio is severely limited in what it can automate without Visual Basic, the template allows a somewhat easier approach – though for this to work, you must ensure that the page-properties are properly set up (see *Add a new page* above).

To define a new business-system on the model:

- identify the name of the business-system
- select a colour to represent the business-system
- add the name and colour to the page-properties:
  - open the properties-sheet for the page itself: right-click on a blank area of the page, then select 'Shape > Custom Properties…'
  - add the name of the business-system to the list in the 'syslist' property: at the end of the existing text-string, enter a semicolon (';'), then the name
  - add the colour-number for the respective colour to the list in the 'syscolour' property: at the end of the existing text-string, enter a semicolon (';'), then the colour-number – either the number shown in the 'Format > Fill… : Color' pull-down, otherwise Visio assigns numbers 24 and above in sequence for the custom-defined colours
- drag a 'Business system' object onto the page, and double-click to define its properties:
  - Name: the name you've entered in the page's 'syslist' list
  - Bus-system: pick the business-system name from the pull-down list
  - (other properties as appropriate)

When you close the object-properties, the new business-system object should be in the correct colour. (If not, check the 'syscolour' list in the page-properties.)

You can now assign Activity objects to the new business-system:

- double-click on an Activity to access its properties
- select the required business-system from the 'Bus-system' pull-down list

Once you've done this for all Activity objects, you should have a complete Business System overview-model – a Function Model colour-coded for the respective business-systems. The next stage – building detail-models for each Business System – is outside the scope of what this template will do, but it does at least provide a place to start.

Map service interdependencies

The template includes a 'Dependency' shape for modelling systemic interdependencies between business functions and activities. The shape directly supports the interdependencies of the extended version of Stafford Beer's 'Viable System Model' described in this book.

Note that each function or activity is likely to have several inter-dependencies – maybe a dozen or more in some cases. To prevent the dependency-model becoming cluttered and unreadable, the usual recommendation is to create a copy of the function-model on a new page, and model the dependencies of only a few activities on each copy – all members of a given Business System, perhaps, or maybe only one at a time.

- drag a 'Dependency' shape onto to the page
- attach its arrowed end to any appropriate connection-point on the reference or 'requester' Function rectangle – i.e. the activity whose dependencies are being modelled
- drag and attach its non-arrowed end to an appropriate connect-point the source or 'provider' Function rectangle – i.e. the activity providing the required service
- double-click on the connection-line to define its properties:
  - Type: type of service provided
  - Name: *optional* name or description to display
  - Comments: *optional* comments for inclusion in reports

The above assumes that arrow-direction indicates direction of service-provision. To align with UML notions of dependency-modelling, assign the opposite arrow-direction – i.e. arrowed end to 'provider', non-arrowed end to 'requester'.

Note that the display-name is constructed automatically from the properties. If you overwrite the text, recreate the link as for the 'Name' property in the Function-object as above.

GLOSSARY

This section summarises some of the key terms and acronyms used in the book.

appropriate matching the intended overall purpose; a *REAL / LEARN* effectiveness-assessment theme associated with the *aspirational dimension* of the context

aspirational dimension aspirational and intentional aspects of work and the workplace, expressed in collective and individual identity and purpose, and in issues such as ethics, values and codes of conduct; also commitment-assets and aspirational capital such as organisational morale, health and fitness

conceptual dimension mental and conceptual aspects of work and the workspace: beliefs, attitudes, knowledge, procedures and process specifications; also knowledge-assets and intellectual capital

effective 'on purpose', producing the intended overall result with an *optimised* balance over the whole; requires broad generalist awareness of the whole, rather than the narrow focus required to create local efficiency, hence often contrasted with *efficient*; see also *REAL/LEARN*

efficient 'doing more with less', creating the maximum result with minimum use or wastage of resources in a specific activity or context; improved incrementally through *active learning* and related techniques for feedback and reflection, although major improvements usually require a change in paradigm; a *REAL/LEARN* theme associated with the *conceptual dimension* of the context

elegant human dimensions of *effectiveness*, such as feelings, emotions and ergonomics, expressed in issues such as usability, simplicity and personal preference; a *REAL / LEARN* effectiveness-assessment theme associated with the *relational dimension* of the context

emergence context within which cause-effect patterns can be identified only retrospectively, and in which analytic techniques are usually unreliable and misleading

enterprise architecture	a systematic process to model and guide *integration* and *optimisation* of the entire enterprise
FEAF	acronym for Federal Enterprise Architecture Framework, a framework and methodology developed for *enterprise architecture* by the US government
goal	a specific objective to be achieved by a specified point in time; emphasis on the behavioural or *physical dimension* of *purpose*, contrasted with *mission, role* and *vision*
integration	contextual awareness of all the interactions between the *physical, conceptual, relational* and *aspirational* dimensions of work and the workspace, and the active process of linking them together into a unified whole
mission	a desired capability or state to be achieved, usually within a specified timeframe, and to be maintained indefinitely once achieved; emphasis on the *emotional* and, to a lesser extent, the *conceptual dimensions* of *purpose*, contrasted with *goal, role* and *vision*
narrative	personalised and often emotive expression or interpretation of knowledge, as history, anecdote or story; link-theme between *mental dimension* and *relational dimension*
optimisation	process of *integration* in which *efficiency* in different areas is traded-off and balanced for maximum *effectiveness* over the whole, between different layers and sub-contexts such as departments, business processes and business units
physical dimension	physical aspects of work and the workspace: skills, competencies, physical processes, behaviours, actions; also tangible assets and work-environment
principle	a conceptual or aspirational commitment or model, the *conceptual-dimension* or *aspirational-dimension* equivalent of *value*
purpose	an expression of individual and/or collective identity - the *aspirational* theme of "who we are and what we stand for"; incorporates distinct dimensions of *vision, role, mission* and *goal*
R^5	collective term for five complexity-science principles used with the *tetradian*, namely *recursion, rotation, reflexion, reciprocation* and *resonance*.
REAL/ LEARN	acronym for four keywords to evaluate effectiveness: *reliable, efficient, appropriate, elegant*; the LEARN acronym includes *integration* in the evaluation-set

145

reciprocation	overall balance in transactions, especially *power-* transactions; reciprocal balance between entities may not be direct or immediate, and in many cases balance may only be achieved over time at a system-wide level, with energy-transfers occurring between *physical, conceptual, relational* and/or *aspirational* dimensions; an R^5 principle for assessment of *effectiveness* and relevance
recursion	patterns of relationship or interaction repeat or are 'self-similar' at different scales; permits simplification of otherwise complex processes; an R^5 principle for assessment of *effectiveness* and relevance
reflexion	corollary of *recursion*, in that the whole, or aspects of the whole, can be identified within the attributes and transactions of any part at any scale; an R^5 principle for assessment of *effectiveness* and relevance
relational dimension	relational and emotional aspects of the work context: feelings and *values*, internal relationships and interpersonal transactions, relationships with external stakeholders; also assets such as reputation and trust
reliable	high degree of certainty and predictability for a desired outcome; a *REAL / LEARN* effectiveness-assessment theme associated with the *physical dimension* of the context
resonance	concept of positive- or negative-feedback (increasing or damping) in a system; permits simplification of otherwise complex processes; an R^5 principle for assessment of *effectiveness* and relevance
rotation	systematic process of assessing a context from multiple perspectives; an R^5 principle for assessment of *effectiveness* and relevance
role	a declared focus or *strategic* position within the 'world' described by a *vision*; emphasis on the *conceptual* and, to a lesser extent, the *relational dimensions* of *purpose*, contrasted with *goal, mission* and *vision*
scenario	an imagined future context, developed for the purpose of understanding both the present context and options for action in the future context
strategy	'big picture' view of an action-plan for an organisation to implement a *purpose*, usually emphasizing its *vision, role* and *mission* components; contrasted with the *tactics* required to execute the plan

146

tactics	detailed *missions, goals* and other step-by-step activities to execute a *strategy*, or some segment of an overall strategy
tetradian	depiction of the *physical, conceptual, relational* and *aspirational* dimensions of a context as four axes in a tetrahedral relationship, usually also showing the respective link-themes as the edges between the vertices of the tetrahedron
TOGAF	acronym for The Open Group Architecture Framework, an IT-oriented framework and methodology for *enterprise architecture* developed collectively by members of the Open Group consortium
value	an emotional commitment
vision	description of a desired 'world', always far greater than any individual or organization; described in the present tense, yet is never 'achieved'; emphasis on the *aspirational dimension* of *purpose*, contrasted with *goal, mission* and *role*; also link-theme between *aspirational dimension* and *relational dimension*
visioning	generic term for the process of identifying, developing and documenting *vision* and *values*, leading towards *strategy* and *tactics*
Zachman framework	a systematic structure for categorisation of models within an IT-oriented *enterprise architecture*, developed by John Zachman

Printed in the United Kingdom by
Lightning Source UK Ltd., Milton Keynes
138446UK00002B/88/P